MAPWISE

UNDERSTANDING MAPS AND DIAGRAMS

Roger Robinson and Ian Jackson

CONTENTS

MAP READING SKILLS	**2**
From photograph to map	2
Finding and measuring	6
Conventional signs	12
The third dimension	16
Landforms	26
Settlements	28
Describing landscape	33
Map interpretation	34
Games and puzzles	40–41

DIAGRAMS, MAPS AND DATA	**48**
Blocks and crosses	49
Cycles and flows	52
Circular diagrams and more systems	56
Land use maps and sketches	58
Models and zones	60
Maps and pictures	62
Density and dots	66

Circles and pyramids	68
Lines and flows	70
Photographs and sketches	72
News and views	74

EXAMINATION QUESTIONS (GCSE STYLE)	**76**
ANSWERS AND COMMENTS	**78**

MAP EXTRACTS

between pages 40 and 41

1	1:50 000 Gloucester	9	1:50 000 Braunton
2	1:25 000 Gloucester	10	1:25 000 Croyde
3	1:50 000 Dartmoor	11	1:50 000 Sevenoaks
4	1:63 360 Dartmoor	12	1:10 000 Key Sheet
5	1:50 000 Key Sheet	13	1:50 000 Tebay
6	1:50 000 Gateshead	14	1:50 000 Craven Arms
7	1:25 000 Langdale	15	1:50 000 Maldon
8	1:25 000 Key Sheet	16	1:25 000 Mynydd Preseli

MAP READING SKILLS

Fig. 1 The River Severn valley west of Gloucester. A vertical air photograph taken from a height of 3 000 m. This photograph was taken several years after the map in Fig. 2 was drawn.

From photograph...

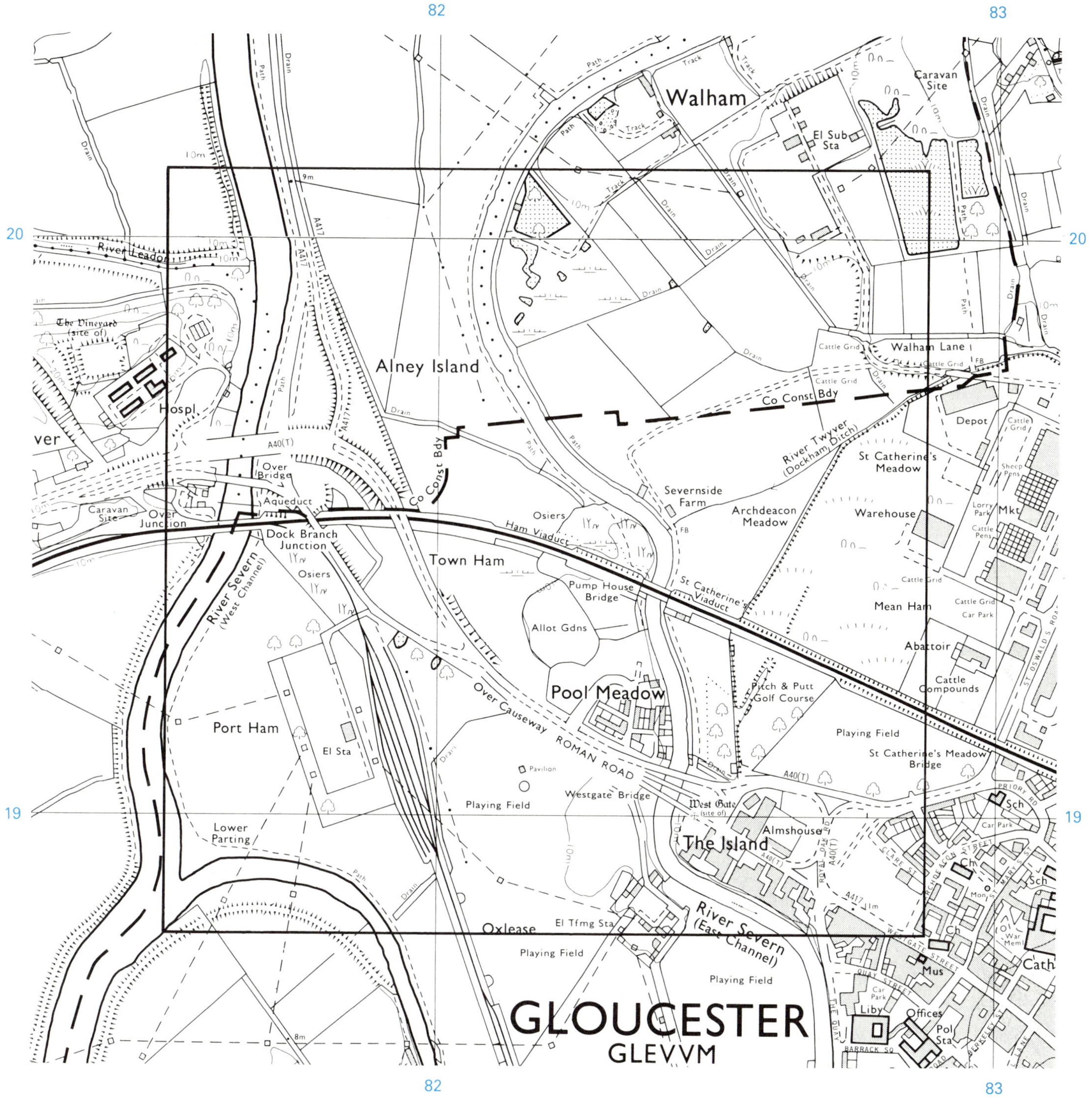

Fig. 2 A large scale map (1:10 000) including the area in Fig. 1. A map is an imaginary view from vertically above the ground. The key sheet is on Map Extract 12 between pages 40 and 41.

Smaller scale maps – less detail

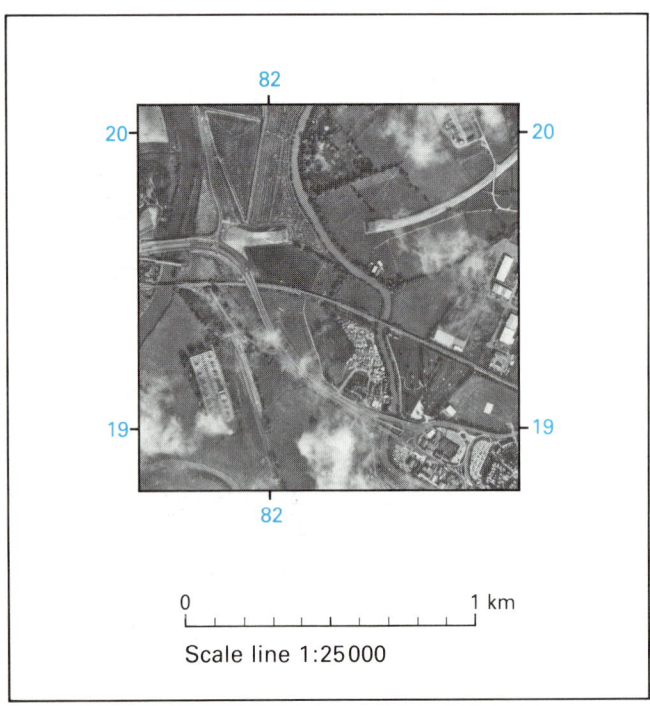

Fig. 3a Vertical air photograph NW of Gloucester, scale 1:25 000.

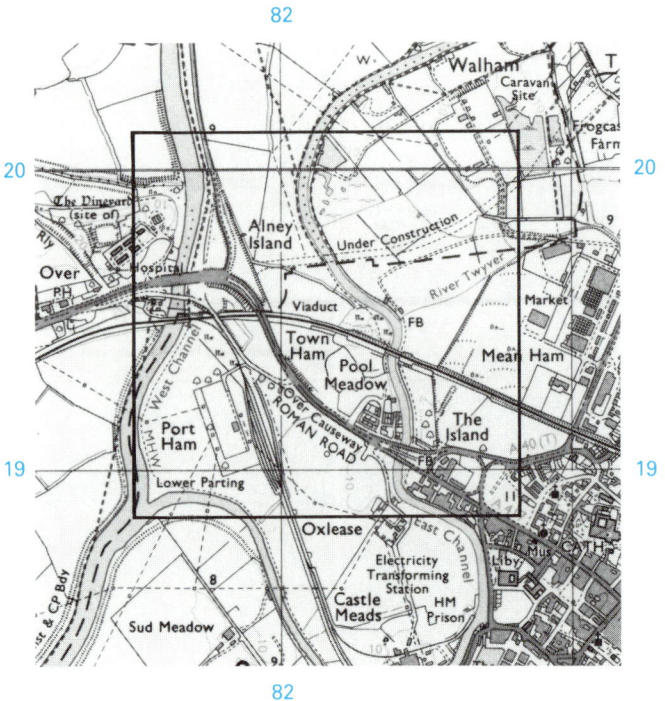

Fig. 3b Map 1:25 000 (part of Map Extract 2).

Most small scale Ordnance Survey maps have a grid of one kilometre squares overprinted on them. The grid lines are numbered in the margins at the edge of each map.

A grid square is named by the two lines that cross at its south-west (bottom left-hand) corner. You always go across the map first when working out the reference, and then up (just as in graphs in mathematics, you give the x co-ordinate before the y co-ordinate). The photograph covers most of square 8219 – i.e. 82 across, 19 up.

Comparing map and photograph
Study Figs. 1 and 2 on pages 2 and 3.
1. Make a list of 10 things that you can see on the photograph **and** on the map.
2. Six that are on the photograph but **not** on the map.
3. Six that are on the map but **not** on the photograph.

The scale of maps
The scale of the map in Fig. 3 is shown by a **scale line**. The scale line is divided up to show what distances on the map mean on the ground.

Each map also has a **statement** of its scale. In Fig. 3 this is 1:25 000 (1 to 25 000). This means that one of any unit of measurement on the map represents 25 000 of the **same** unit in reality. 1 cm on the map represents 25 000 cm in reality.

The scale can be given as a **representative fraction**. This is the same really as a scale statement, so 1:25 000 is an RF of 1/25 000.

4. Look at Fig. 3. Measure along the scale line to find out how far 1 cm on the map is on the ground.
5. Make a scale statement and an RF for the map.
6. Look at Fig. 4; the scale is 1:50 000. What distance would 1 cm represent in reality?
7. Check your answer on the scale line.

The areas covered by maps
The map in Fig. 3 is twice the scale of the one in Fig. 4. In Fig. 4 1 km is 2 cm, in Fig. 3 1 km is 4 cm. But you can see that the size of the photo on Fig. 3 is 4 times that on Fig. 4!

The relationship between scale and the size of a map is complex (if you increase the scale by x, you increase the size of the map by x squared).

When you are using maps it is important just to know that changes in scale are different from changes in the size of maps or in the area they cover.

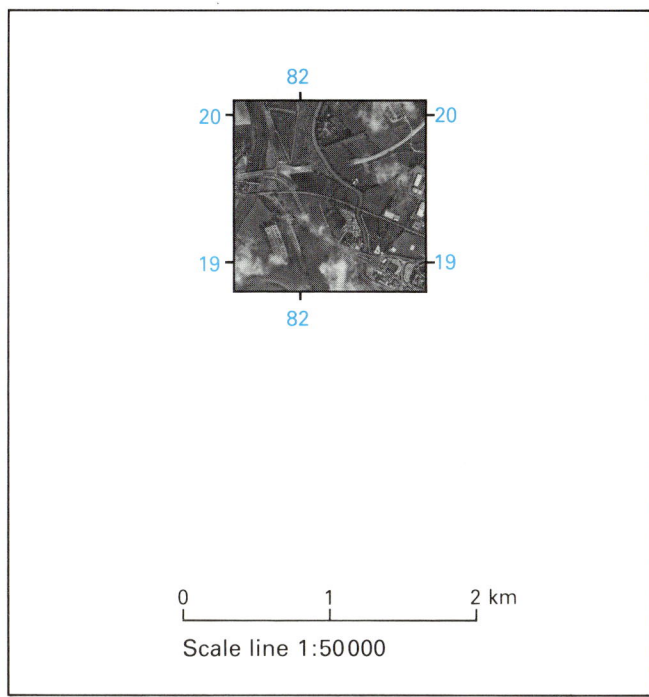

Fig. 4a Vertical air photograph, scale 1:50 000.

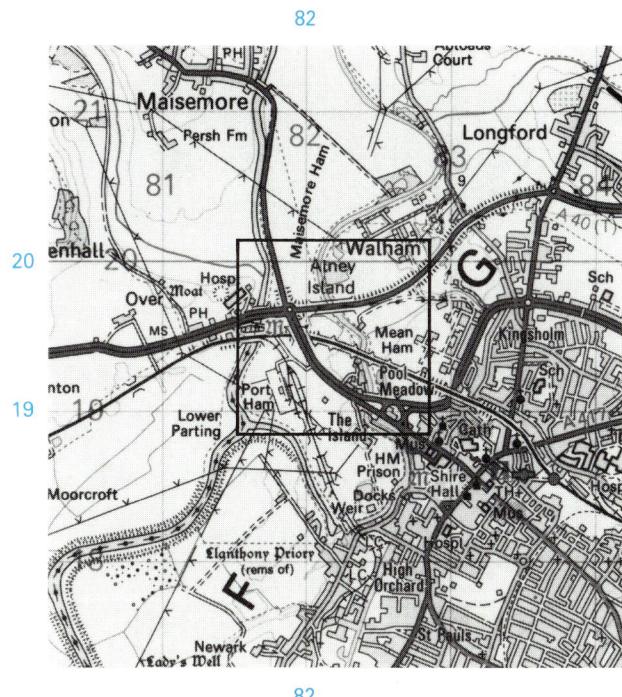

Fig. 4b Map 1:50 000 (part of Map Extract 1).

The language of maps

Maps are made up of lines, shapes, shading, symbols and words. The Key Sheets (Map Extracts 5, 8 and 12) show the meaning of all these on OS maps, Exercises 8 to 15 explore this 'map language'.

Open out Map Extract 2 and put a marker in the page for the Key Sheet (Map Extract 8).

8 Pick out as many **lines** as you can on the Fig. 3a photograph and use the map and key to make sure what they are (e.g. field boundary, river, etc.).

9 There are many **lines** on the map that are imaginary (e.g. grid lines, contours to show the height and shape of the land, administrative boundaries). Find an administrative boundary on Map Extract 2 and say what it means.

10 Make a list of some obvious **shapes** from the Fig. 3a photograph and make sure what they are (e.g. buildings, fields, woods, etc.).

11 Many shapes are **shaded** to make them easier to identify. What is the colour of the shading used for buildings?

12 Choose six **symbols** from the map that represent things that can be seen on the photograph (churches, bridges, etc.). Write down their meanings.

13 List all the **words and letters** used on Map Extract 2 on the area covered by the photograph.

14 Underline the **words** in your list that are 'place names'. What different styles and sizes of print are used? Why?

15 Write down the meanings of the other **words and letters** in your list.
(Save your answers to 10 and 12 for later work.)

Now do the same exercises using the 1:50 000 map (Map Extract 1) and its Key Sheet (Map Extract 5). Call the exercises 8a to 15a to avoid confusion.

16 Compare the 1:25 000 with the 1:50 000 map: write a paragraph explaining what you think are the main differences between the maps and the information you can get from them.

Finding and measuring

The National Grid

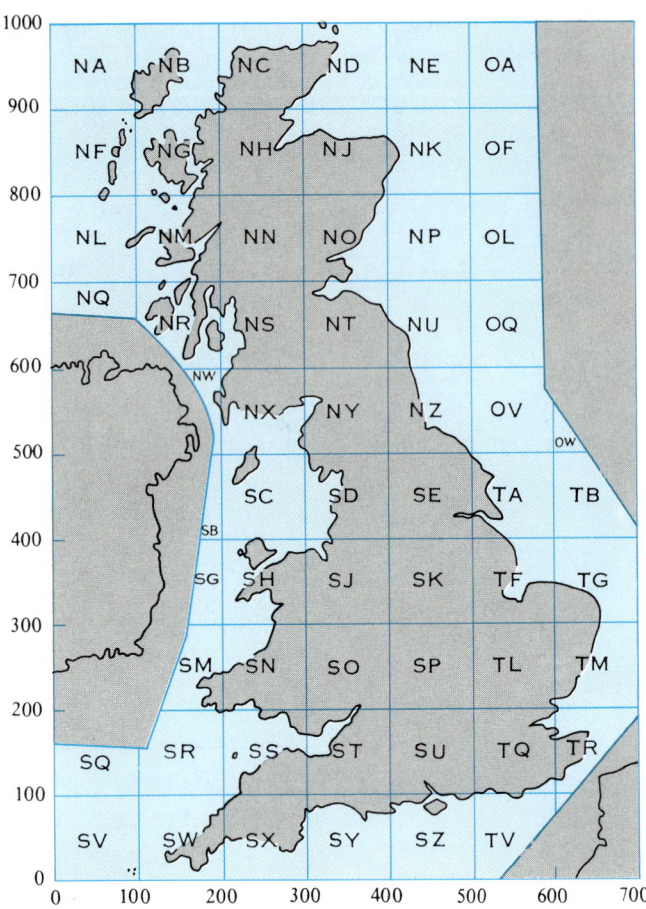

Fig. 5 The National Grid and 100 km squares.

The Ordnance Survey maps use the National Grid shown on Fig. 5. Each big square on Fig. 5 is 100 km by 100 km, and each is given a label of two letters. So the area around Gloucester in Figs. 3 and 4 is part of 100 km square SO.

OS large scale maps and plans (1:25 000, 1:10 000, 1:2 500, 1:1 250) all use this reference system to name the map sheets that you can buy. The 1:50 000 map sheets have their own numbering system, from 1 in northern Scotland to 204 in SW England. The key for these sheets is printed on the back of OS 1:50 000 folded maps.

1 Why do you think the grid was produced?
2 Why are the 100 km squares lettered?

Grid references

10 km grid squares

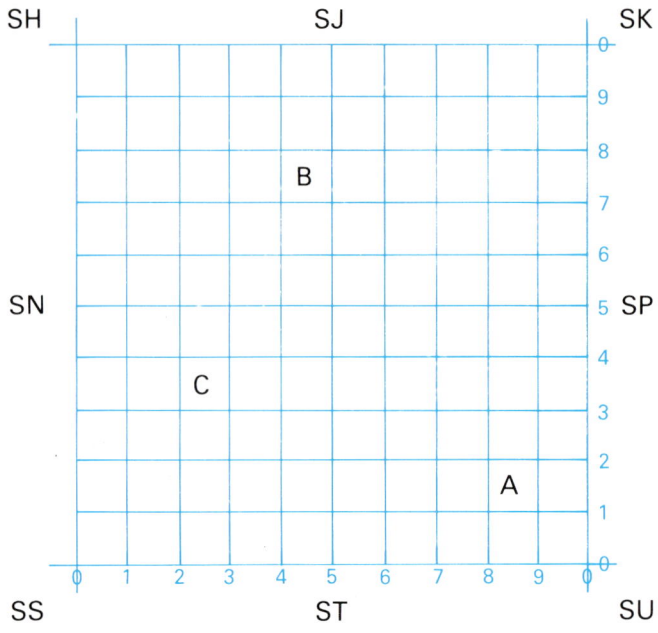

Fig. 6 The 100 km grid square SO divided into one hundred 10 km squares.

Each 100 km grid square is divided into one hundred 10 km squares, and Fig. 6 shows how each 10 km square has a reference. These are used as the labels for the 1:25 000 map sheets on sale.

3 Look back at the explanation on page 4 of how labels are worked out for 1 km grid squares.
Remember always easting **before** northing (E is before N in the alphabet, or you must go along the hall, before going up the stairs!)
On Fig. 6 the 10 km square marked A is called SO 81, square B is SO 47. What is square C?

Four-figure grid references

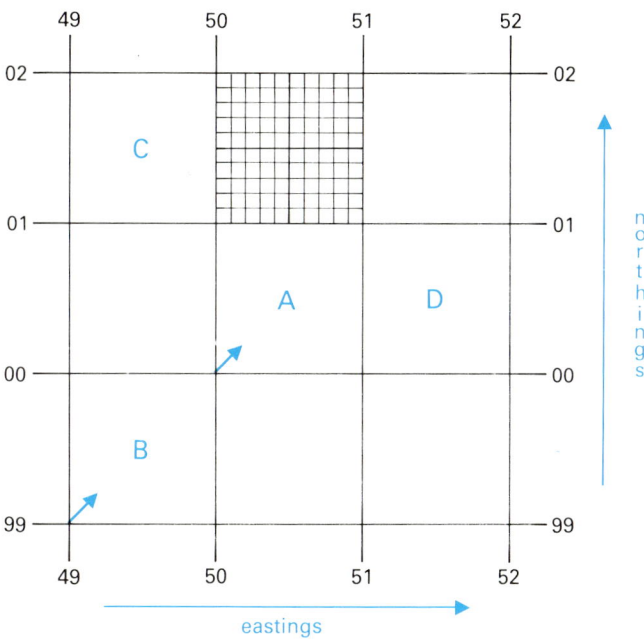

Fig. 7 One kilometre grid squares.

Each 10 km square in Fig. 6 is divided up again into 1 km squares that are marked by grid lines which are numbered on OS maps. Four-figure grid references are used to locate a 1 km square, and guide you to the SW corner of a square.

4 In Fig. 7, kilometre grid square A is 50 east, 00 north (written as 5000). Square B is 4999. What are the four-figure references for squares C and D?

Six-figure grid references

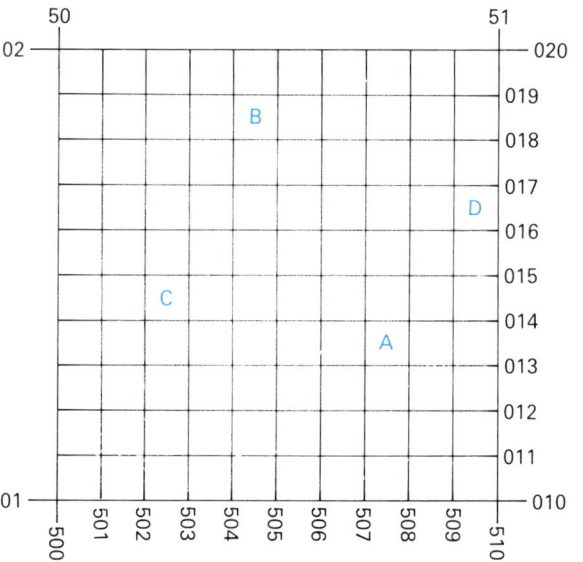

Fig. 8 A 1 km grid square divided into 100 squares each 100 m by 100 m.

These guide you to a particular place inside a one kilometre square. In Fig. 7, square 5001 is divided up into 100 squares each 100 m by 100 m. Fig. 8 shows the numbers used for the imaginary grid lines. Where they cross locates the SW corner of a square – this time the square is only 100 m by 100 m.

5 In Fig. 8 the reference for A is easting grid line 50 and seven-tenths, written as 507. The northing is line 01 and three-tenths – 013. This gives a six figure reference of 507013 for A. B is 504018. What are the six-figure references for C and D?

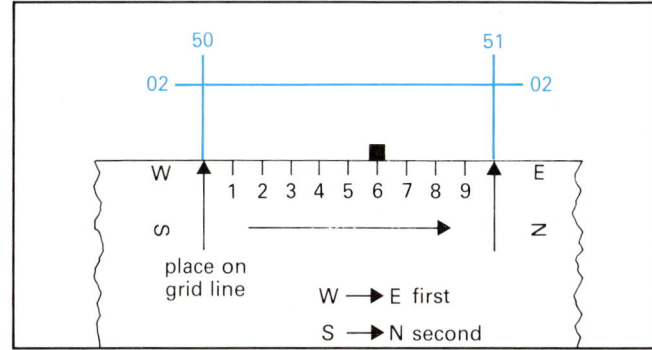

Fig. 9a Scale for 1:25 000 maps. This 'building' has an easting of 506.

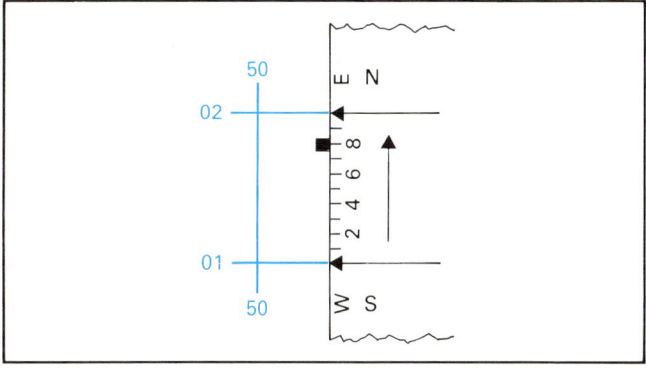

Fig. 9b Scale for 1:50 000 maps. This 'building' has a northing of 018.

You can use scales like those in Fig. 9 to help estimate the tenths. Draw the scale for the map you are using (on the edge of a piece of card) and place it across the grid square you are looking at.

6 Look back at your answers to questions 10 and 12 from page 5. Use Map Extract 2 to give a six-figure GR for each item on your list for 10 and 12. (For more GR practice turn to page 40.)

A **full** grid reference puts the letters of the 100 km square (as on Fig. 5) in front of the six-figure reference.

This is explained on each OS map sheet. An example is given inside the back cover of this book.

7 Use a local map to find your home's full GR.

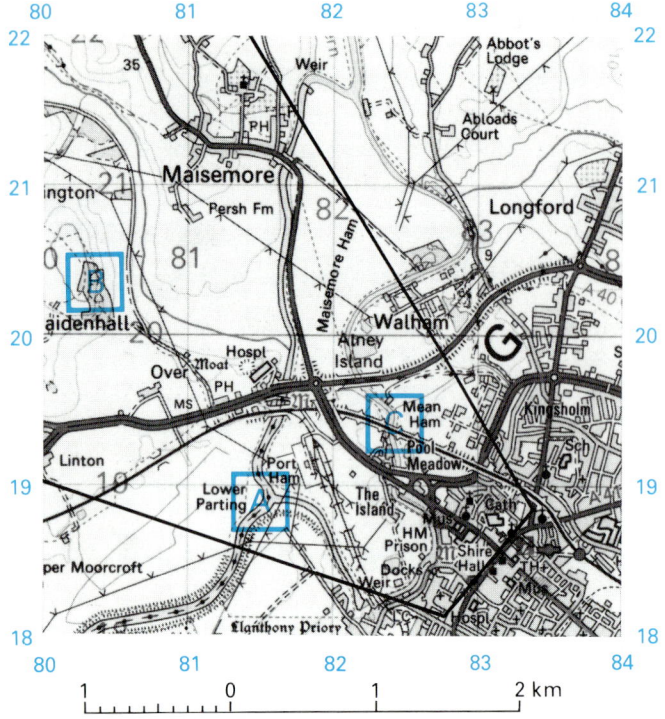

Fig. 10 Map showing view for Fig. 11.

Distances

Distance is not easy to judge without practice. The oblique photograph in Fig. 11 is more difficult to relate to a map than the vertical photograph (Fig. 1). But it is the kind of view we can get from a hill-top.

1. Looking at the photograph **only**, how far do you think it is from (i) A to B (ii) B to C and (iii) C to A?
2. Use Fig. 10 to check the distances between A, B and C using the scale line.
3. The six-figure references around the photograph refer to (i) deciduous wood (ii) cathedral (iii) an unfenced road (iv) a railway viaduct over a river (v) a large road junction (vi) Port Ham (vii) a hospital (viii) a river confluence (ix) docks (x) a prison (xi) Maisemore (xii) a railway freight line (xiii) a road bridge over a railway.

   Use the photograph and Map Extracts 1 and 2. Write down (i) to (xiii) and decide which GR goes with each.
4. Using the grid squares on Extract 2 estimate to the nearest half kilometre the distance between (i) and (ii), (ii) and (x), and (vii) and (ix).

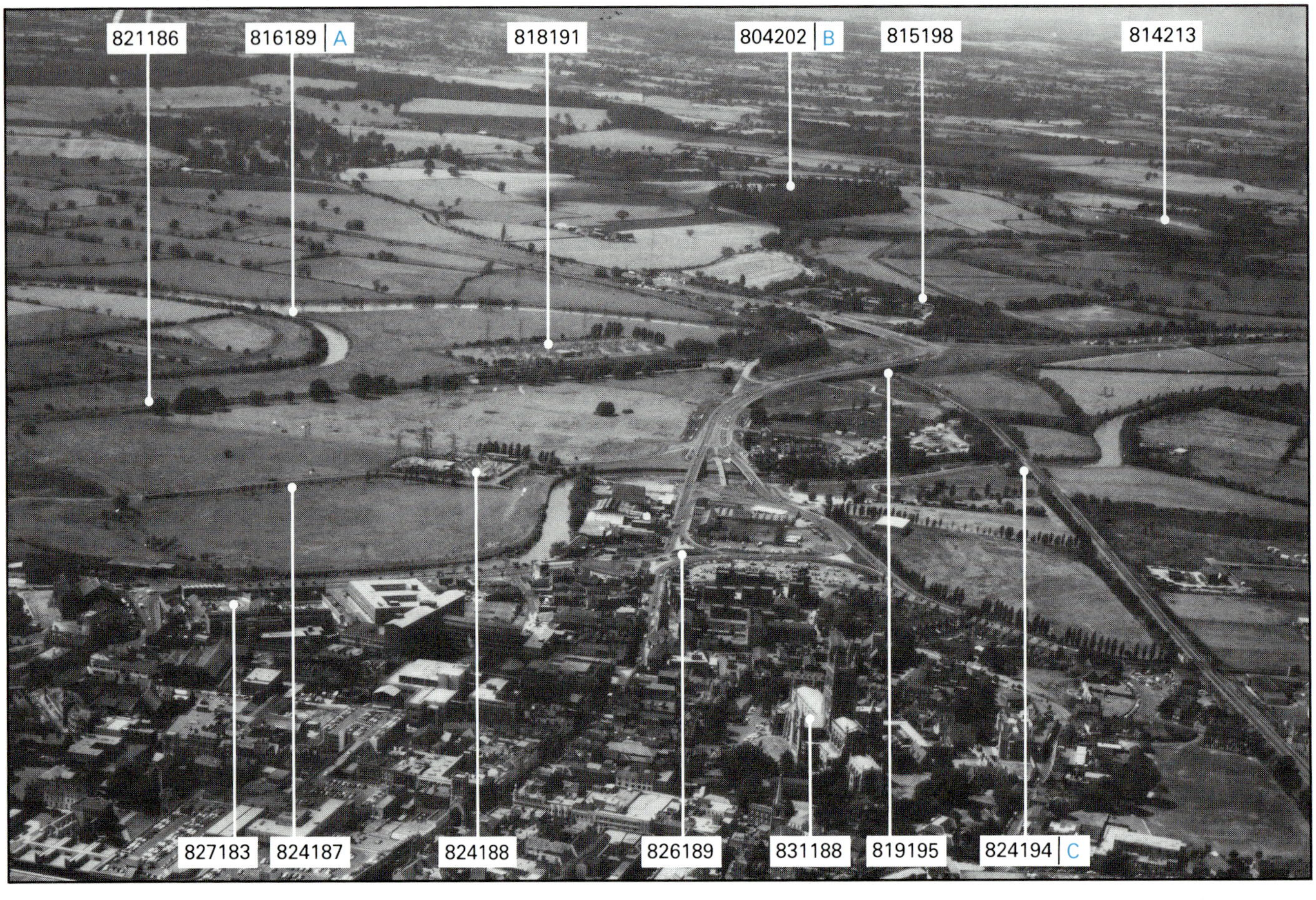

Fig. 11 Oblique air photograph looking north-west from Gloucester.

Straight line distances

Using a scale line

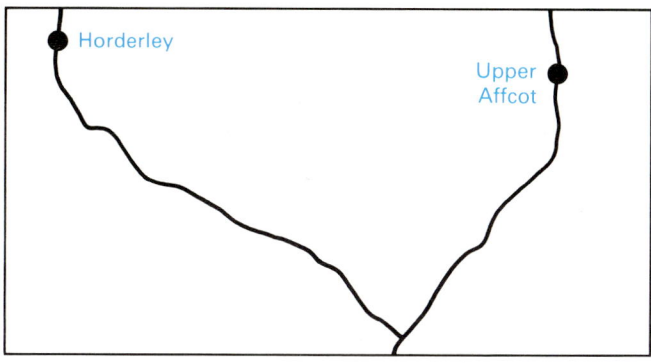

Fig. 12a Distance between Horderley and Upper Affcot.

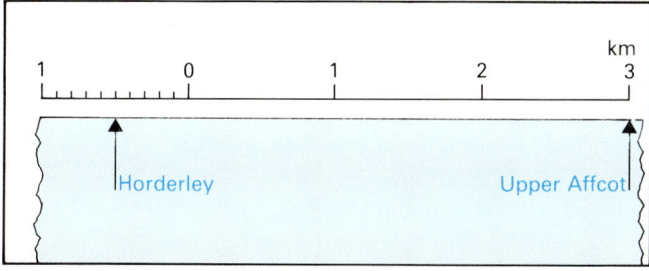

Fig. 12b Using a scale line. Horderley is 3 km and 500 m from Upper Affcot.

The easiest way to measure straight line distances is to mark off the distance on the straight edge of a piece of paper held on the map. Then measure the length against a scale line.

Scale lines are found in the margin of OS maps.

Using a ruler

Measure the distance on the map in cm – Horderley to Upper Affcot is 7 cm. Convert this to distance in reality by multiplying by the scale factor – in Fig. 12 this is 1:50 000. So 7 cm × 50 000 = 350 000 cm. Divide by 100 to get metres (= 3 500 m), then by 1 000 to get kilometres (= 3.5 km).

Look at Map Extract 14 (Craven Arms, Shropshire).
1 Find the straight line distances (to the nearest half km) between the following places and each of the others:
Acton Scott (4589); Craven Arms (4382); Hopesay (3983); Moorwood (4585); Hamperley (4189).

Travel distances

To find the distance travelled along a route you can follow the bends and turns on the map using a piece of string or cotton, or by marking off sections on the straight edge of a piece of paper. (Do not try to measure bending routes with a ruler, it is likely to be very inaccurate.)

Measure the string or the distance along the edge of the paper on the scale line.

2 What is the travel distance between Horderley and Henley along the roads marked on Fig. 12?
3 Use Map Extract 14 and find the travel distances on tarred or metalled roads where possible (i.e. all those that are coloured on the 1:50 000 map) between the five places in Exercise 1 on this page.

Time distances

Long distance walking 3 km/hr (+ 1 hour for every 300 m climb)
Short distance walking 4 km/hr (under 4 km)
Long distance cycling 20 km/hr
Car on local roads 50 km/hr
Car on motorways 100 km/hr

Fig. 13 Travel speeds.

Once a travel distance has been measured, the time it will take to do the journey can be estimated. Of course the time depends on the kind of transport (Fig. 13).

4 About how long would it take to cycle from Craven Arms to each of the other four places and back?

Measuring area

Imperial	Metric
square yard = 1 yd × 1 yd (yd²)	square metre = 1 m × 1 m (m²)
acre = 4840 yd² (a) (69.6 yd × 69.6 yd)	hectare = 10 000 m² (ha) (100 m × 100 m)
square mile = 640 acres (sq ml)	square km = 100 hectares (km²)
1 acre is about 0.40 ha 1 sq ml is about 2.5 km²	1 hectare is about 2.5 acres 1 km² is about 0.40 sq ml

Fig. 14 Imperial and metric area measures.

Fig. 15 Areas on maps.

Two kinds of measurement are used in the UK. One is the old **imperial** system, the other is the **metric**. Fig. 14 shows how the two systems work for area.

In this book we use the metric system.

Fig. 15 shows the size some areas would appear.

It is not often necessary to work out an exact area from a map, but it is useful to make estimates. Follow this method:
(i) trace the outline of the area you want to measure;
(ii) put the tracing paper on top of centimetre graph paper (with small squares 1 mm by 1 mm) and count the approximate number of small squares covered by the area;
(iii) change the answer into 'real world' units using this information:
1:10 000 map: 100 small squares (1 cm² = 1 ha)
1:25 000 map: 16 squares = 1 ha (1 cm² = 6 ha)
1:50 000 map: 4 squares = 1 ha (1 cm² = 25 ha).

Look at Map Extract 2.
1 Work out the area of the field with its centre at
   (i) 804168   (ii) 813201   (iii) 825216   (iv) 814182.
2 What is the area of the housing estate at 835200? (Include houses, roads and open space.)

Look at Map Extract 1.
3 What is the area of the woodland at 839253?
4 What is the area of Highnam Court grounds?
5 Using a tracing of Fig. 16, without the pitches marked on it, mark out the games field for the summer season. Choose a site for
   (i) a running track (area needed 170 m by 170 m)
   (ii) a cricket pitch (radius 70 m)
   (iii) a stand (10 m by 50 m).
Mark your choice on the map.

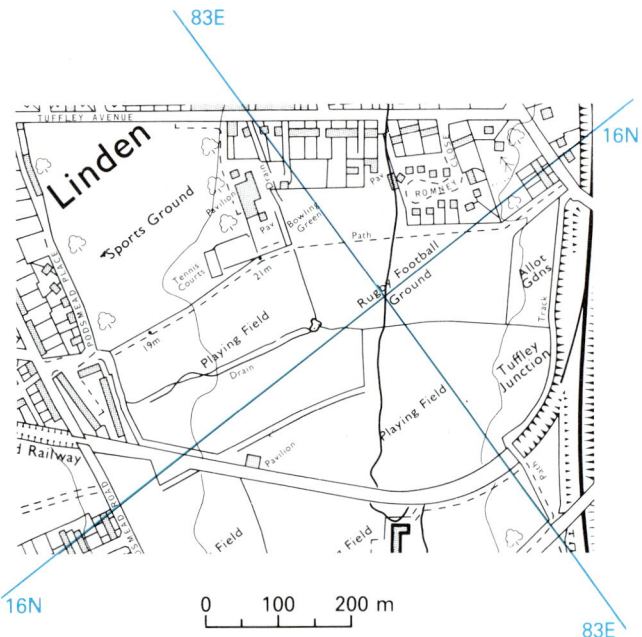

Fig. 16 1:10 000 map of playing fields.

Directions

The compass rose

The four cardinal points of the compass (Fig. 17) are north, east, south and west. (Going clockwise 'Never eat sausages whole'.) The next four points just come between these: NE, SE, SW and NW. The other eight directions can be remembered by moving **away** from NE, SE, SW and NW – so it is 'to the north of NE (NNE)' and 'to the east of NE', and so on.

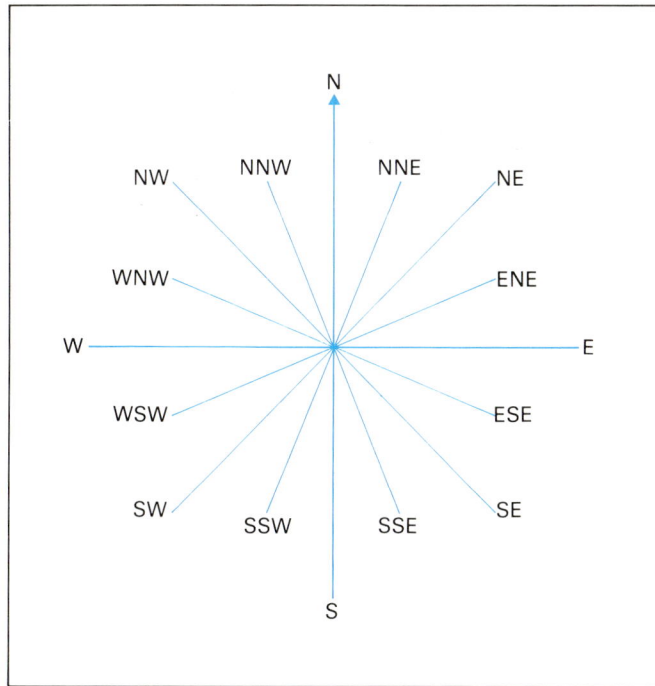

Fig. 17 The compass rose.

North

The direction the compass rose points depends on the direction of north – and there are three 'norths' in common use! They are shown on the top margin of 1:50 000 OS maps (Fig. 18).
 (i) **True north** is the direction to the North Pole where the axis on which the earth spins reaches the surface. The North Pole star is directly above it.
 (ii) **Magnetic north** is the direction to the Magnetic North Pole which moves around the True North Pole.
 (iii) **Grid north** is the direction along the N–S grid lines on a map, and is used for directions around the map.

1 Make a tracing of the compass rose (Fig. 17). Use it with Map Extract 15. Place your rose so that its centre is on GR840110.
  What direction from you is: (i) 840078 (ii) 862110 (iii) 888158 (iv) 817119 (v) 848091?
2 Place your rose on (i) to (v) in turn. What direction is it to your original position from each?
3 Two balloonists lift off from GR860157 and fly 6 km SSE. Where do they land? What do they fly over?
4 Plan a flight giving directions and distances.

Magnetic north is most important when using maps in the field. When you need to line up your map with the countryside, or **orientate** yourself, you need to use a compass and to line up the magnetic north arrow (Fig. 18) with the compass north. In the UK magnetic north in 1985 was about 6° W of grid north, decreasing by 10' each year. (There are 60' in 1°.)

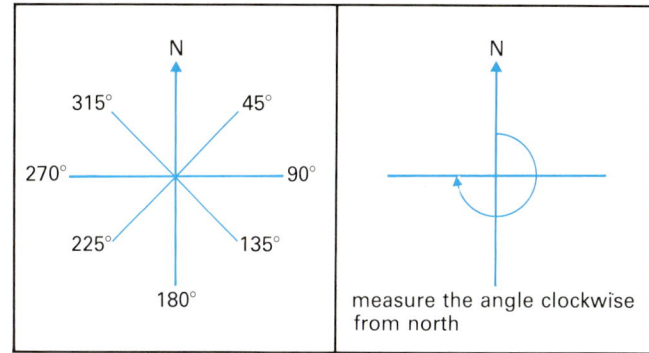

Fig. 19 Compass bearings.

Compass bearings

Directions for walking or navigation are often given in bearings (Fig. 19). The full compass rose is 360° and the bearings are given in degrees east of north, working round in a clockwise direction. East is 90° E of N, west is 270° E of N.

5 Change your answers for Exercise 1 to grid bearings.
6 Rewrite them using magnetic bearings.

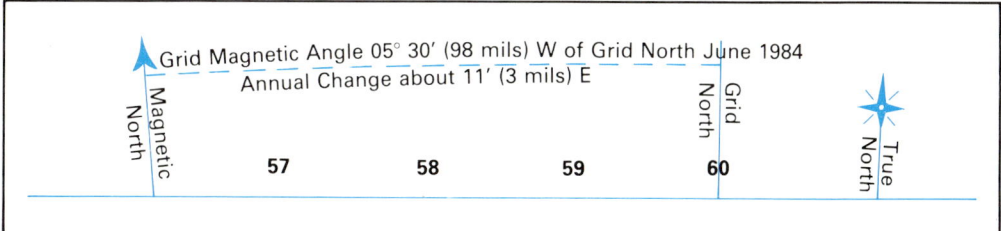

Fig. 18 Three norths: the top margin of OS 1:50 000 map sheet 180.

Conventional signs

The photographs on these pages were taken in an area of Map Extract 10. Fig. 20 shows the location and direction of view for each photograph. The features are shown on OS 1:25 000 maps by conventional signs.

1. Use Map Extract 10 and the key (Map Extract 8) and match the photographs with the conventional signs on the map. Give a six-figure grid reference for each.
2. Look at Map Extract 9 and its key (Map Extract 5). Which of the 10 features are also shown on the 1:50 000 map by conventional signs?
3. Now make up your own exercise by sketching a page like this for a 1:50 000 map. Use nine grid squares from Map Extract 6. Draw the pictures and mark the positions on the grid. Ask your neighbour to do your 'Exercise 1'.

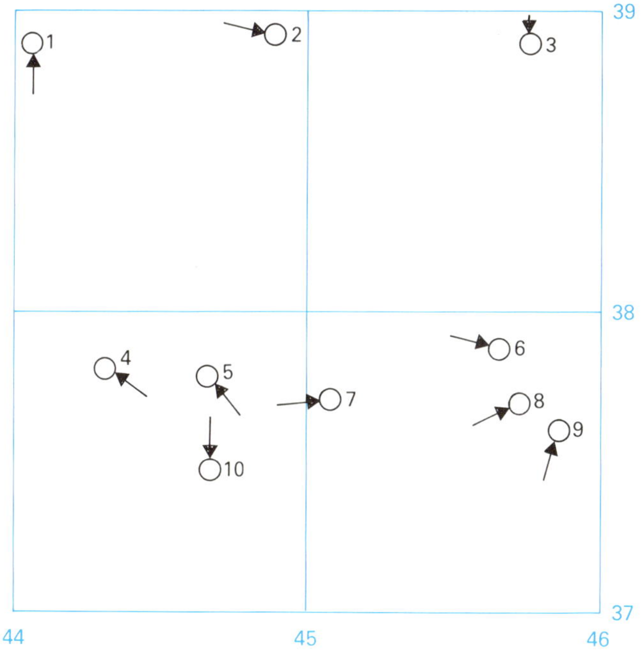

Fig. 20 Part of the grid on Map Extracts 9 and 10.

Study conventional signs

1 This is the story of a day out on Map Extract 14 (Craven Arms). The numbers refer to the conventional signs on Fig. 21. Follow the journey on the map and fill in the 17 blanks.

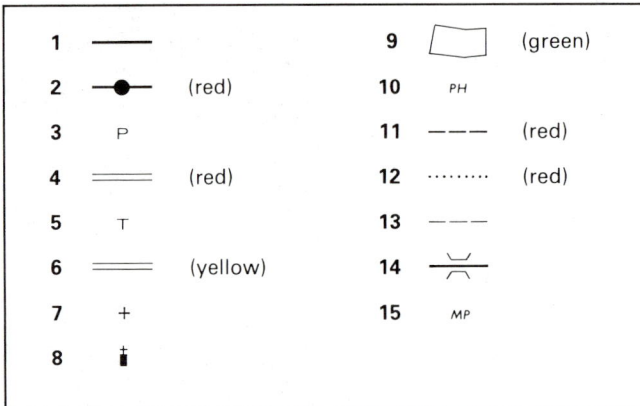

Fig. 21 Selected conventional signs OS 1:50 000 (First Series). For full colours see Map Extract 5 (the colours used on the actual map are named).

We travelled on a (1) and arrived at Craven Arms (GR4382) at 9 a.m. We walked out of the (2) and visited (3) across the (4) to buy a few stamps before catching a bus northwards. We got out at the (5) in grid square 4489, and walked up the (6) for 1.5 km until we came to (7). We had a look at it, then walked a little way back and turned south to find the Farm Museum – but suddenly thunder and lightening crashed about us. We ran to the (8) for shelter. It was locked, but luckily had a big porch. We were glad we weren't in the (9) opposite. The rain eased up and we decided to head back, looking for lunch on the way. We were disappointed that there wasn't a (10) in Acton Scott, but found one near where we got off the bus. We had a snack, and the landlord told us there wasn't a bus back to Craven Arms until 6 p.m. We set out along the (11) to walk back. We missed the (12) and went down a (13), the course of a Roman road. A farmer stopped us and after grumbling about 'rights of way' put us on the right path for The Corner. It seemed a long walk to the A489 where we turned left, went under a (14), turned right at the junction and were pleased to see the (15) that told us it was only (x) km to Craven Arms. We arrived there in (y) minutes.

2 Now choose a map extract and make up your own story of a journey using a diagram like Fig. 21.

Extracting information from maps

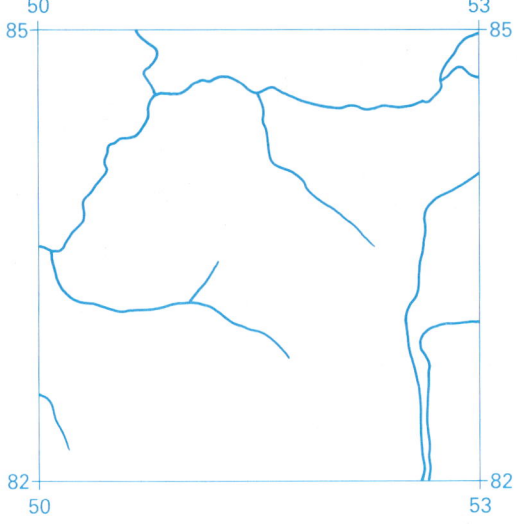

Fig. 22 'Water'.

'Seeing' all the different information on a map is a skill that needs practice. The exercises below help by concentrating on one set of information at a time.

3 On a piece of tracing paper draw four separate squares 6 cm by 6 cm. On Map Extract 3 (Dartmoor, 1:50 000) find the nine grid squares bounded by eastings 50 and 53, and northings 82 and 85.
4 Place your first traced square over this area and trace on all the water shown on the map. Label this map '(A) Water'. It should look like Fig. 22.
5 Do the same on your other traced squares for: (B) Roads (C) Woods and (D) Buildings.
6 Cut up your tracing paper and overlay the tracings two at a time. Which pairs have patterns that match? What links are there between the patterns?
7 Note and try to explain anything that does not seem to fit the general patterns you have found.
8 Do the same exercise for the four grid squares (8 cm by 8 cm) on Map Extract 16 (Preseli Hills, 1:25 000), bounded by eastings 08 and 10, and northings 33 and 35.
9 Choose nine grid squares from a 1:50 000 map. Note the grid line numbers. Choose **one** element to extract from the map as you did before.
10 Exchange tracings with your neighbour. Tell them which map extract you used. Their task is to (i) guess what the element is (ii) locate the nine squares on the map (iii) check your tracing for accuracy.

Make your own map

0 ───────────────────── 1 km

Fig. 23 Vertical air photograph. The river in the tidal estuary flows to the south-west.

1. Put a piece of tracing paper over Fig. 23 and mark in the frame of the photo and the scale line.
2. Mark on the river estuary (coastline) in blue.
3. Add any rivers you can see, also in blue.
4. Mark on roads. Make a key for 'main roads' and 'other roads'.
5. Mark in buildings, make up your own symbols and add them to your key.
6. Mark in any woodland and field boundaries.
7. Choose some names for settlements, rivers, woods, etc. Print them on the map.
8. Add any other information you think is important and make sure your key is complete.

The third dimension

Clues to height

So far we have ignored the ways maps show relief, but all maps do give clues to the shape and height of the land. Some clues are also visible in reality, like the **triangulation point** (Fig. 24). These are used in survey work and are placed on high points so that sightings can be taken between them.

Heights are also shown by **bench marks** and **spot heights** (Fig. 25). All heights are measured in height above mean sea level at Newlyn in Cornwall. Mean sea level is half way between the high and low watermarks shown on maps of coastal areas (Fig. 26).

Look at Map Extract 11.
1. What do you find at: (i) 542599 (ii) 597587?

Relief features like cliffs, embankments, and quarries are shown on OS maps mainly by shading and hachures – some of them are in Fig. 27.

Look at Map Extract 3.
2. In squares 4979 and 5184 are the features cuttings or embankments?
3. What feature is at: (i) 551848 (ii) 521747?

These signs are very good for detail, but the OS rely on **contours** for the general pattern.

A contour is an imaginary line through all points at the same height on the ground.

Any particular contour is exactly level, if you walk along the line of a contour you will not go uphill or downhill at all.

Contours cannot cross each other, and if they seem to join up or come to a stop they have reached a cliff or vertical slope.

The difference in height between one contour and the next one up or down is the **contour interval**.

Fig. 24 Typical weather at the triangulation station (874 m) on Goat Fell, Isle of Arran.

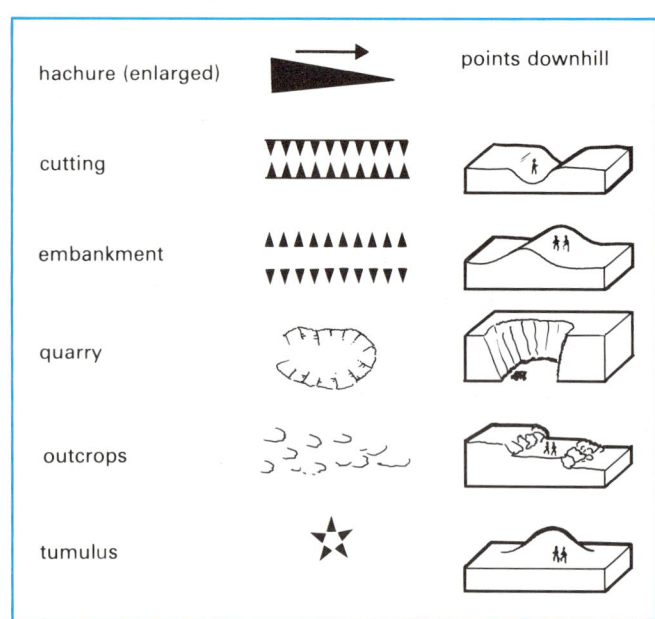

Fig. 27 Relief features.

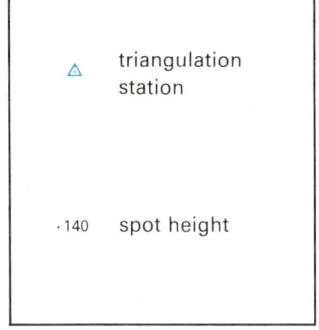

Fig. 25 Heights.

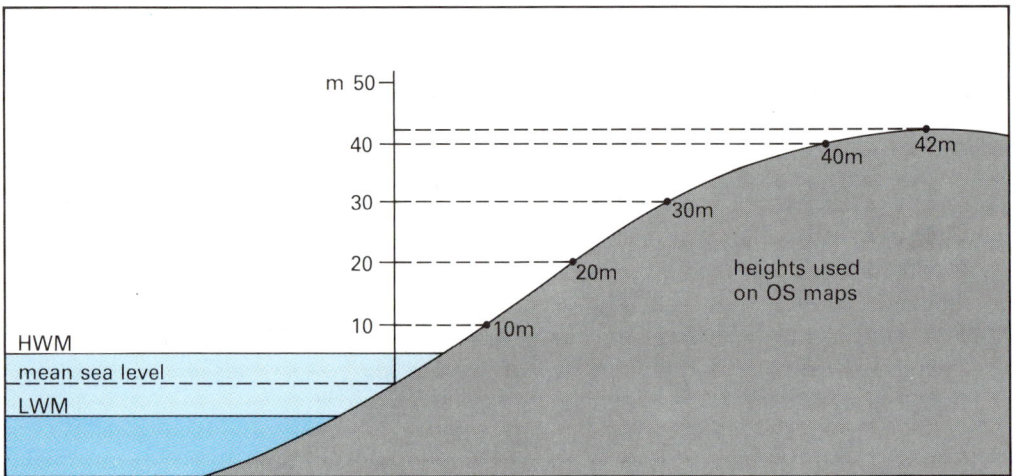

Fig. 26 Mean sea level.

Make your own contours

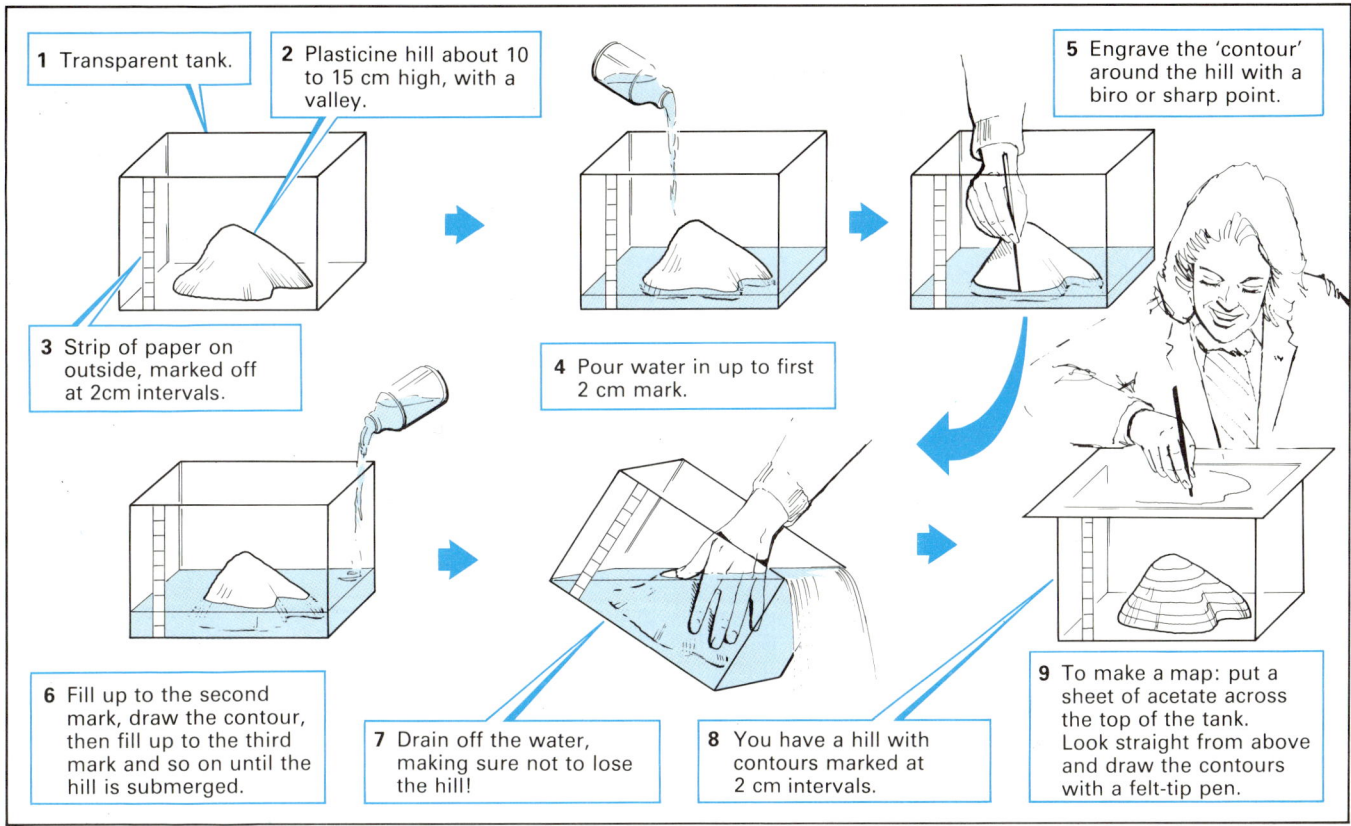

Fig. 28 Make your own contours: class activity.

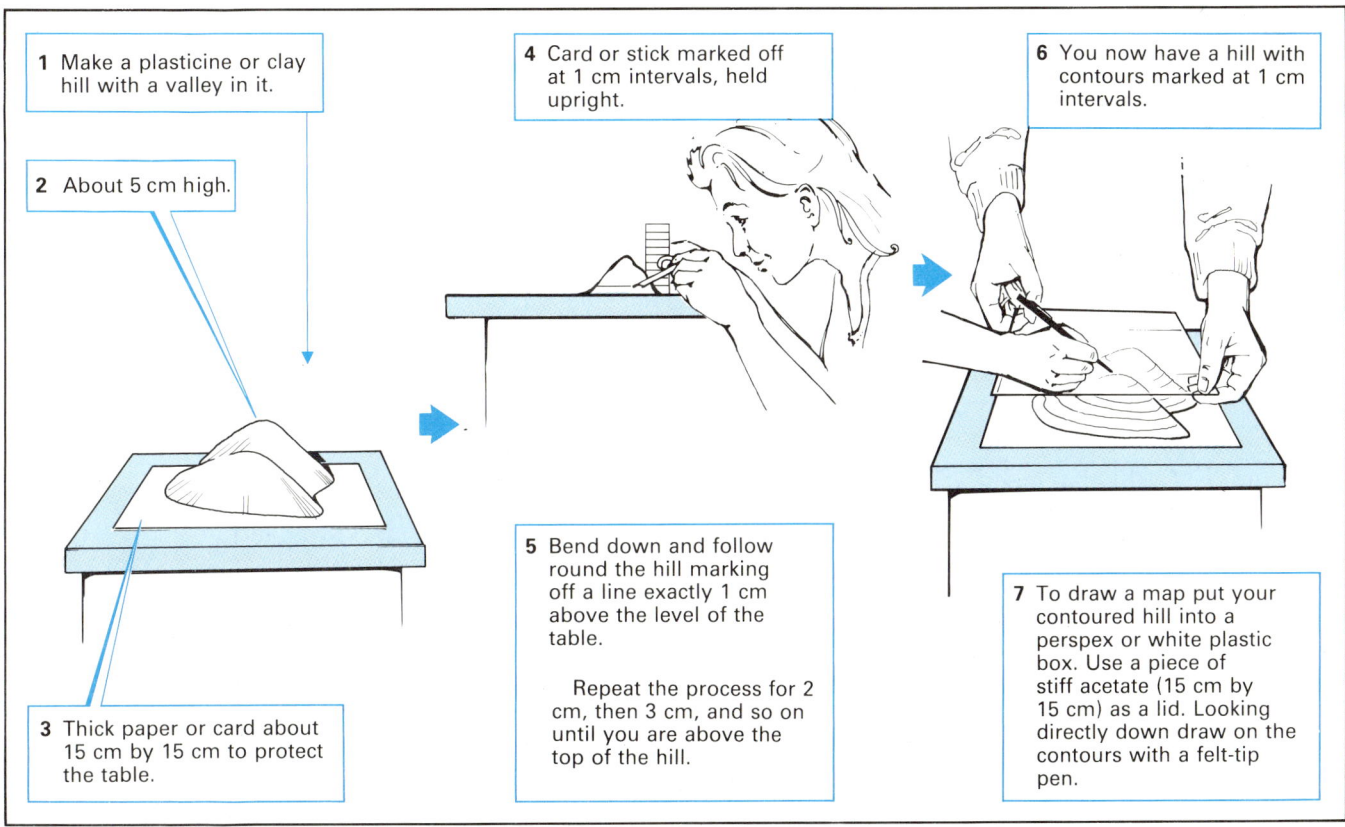

Fig. 29 Make your own contours: group activity.

Asim Island

Asim Island is very small and the block diagrams are drawn by the computer using the same scale vertically and horizontally. They look very like they would in reality.

1. Compare the map (Fig. 30) with Fig. 31. When the contours are closer together on the map is the slope steeper or gentler?
2. Trace Fig. 31, but slice the top off Asim Island at the 30 m contour to leave it with a flat top.

Figs. 32, 33 and 34 are three views of Asim Island. The captions tell you the angle of the viewing point – 0° is horizontal, and a map view is from 90°.

3. Which of the views is from: (i) south (ii) WNW and (iii) NNE?
4. Make a tracing of the map (Fig. 30). Use the block diagrams to help you to mark each of the following features on your tracing (make a key): (i) summit (ii) ridge (iii) spur (iv) valley (v) a small plain (vi) a steep slope (vii) a gentle slope. (These features are described on page 26.)
5. Complete your map by adding: (i) a river and some streams (ii) a landing stage for boats (iii) a footpath to the summit (iv) a seat from which to watch the setting sun.
6. Use a tracing or drawing of one of the block diagrams as the basis for a poster either (a) advertising the island as a great place to visit for a day, or (b) getting support for regulations to stop the island being flooded by visitors.

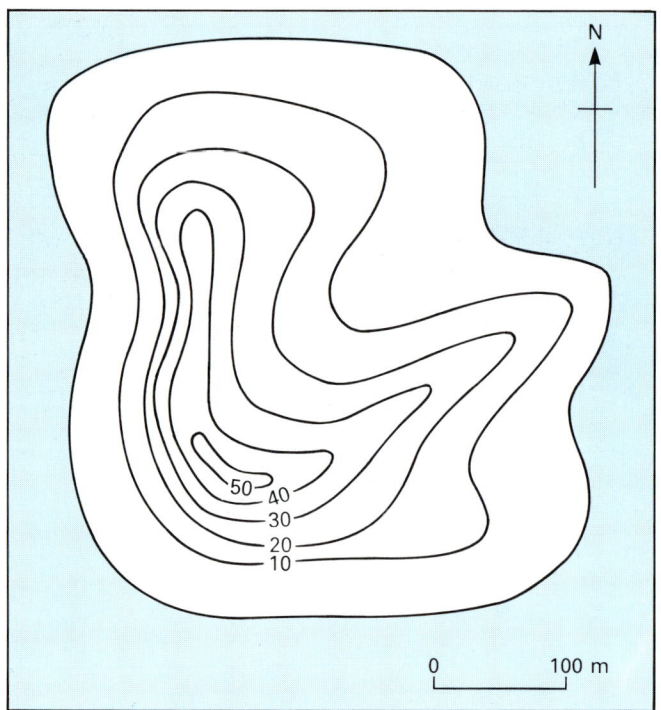

Fig. 30 Asim Island (contours in metres).

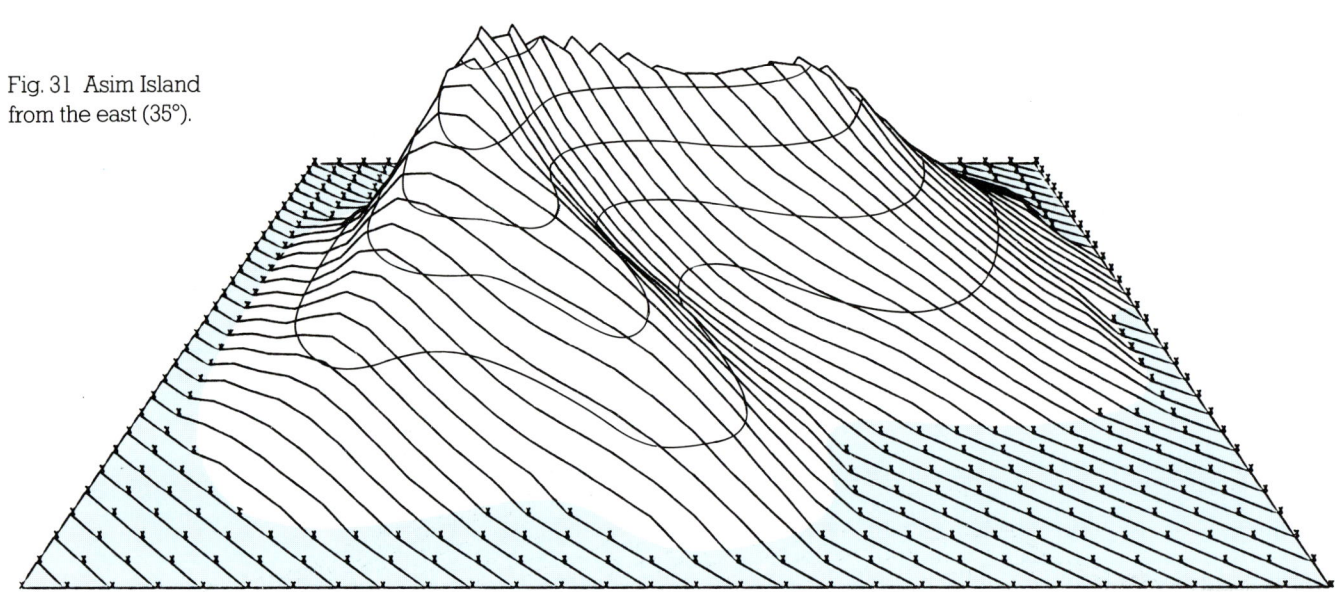

Fig. 31 Asim Island from the east (35°).

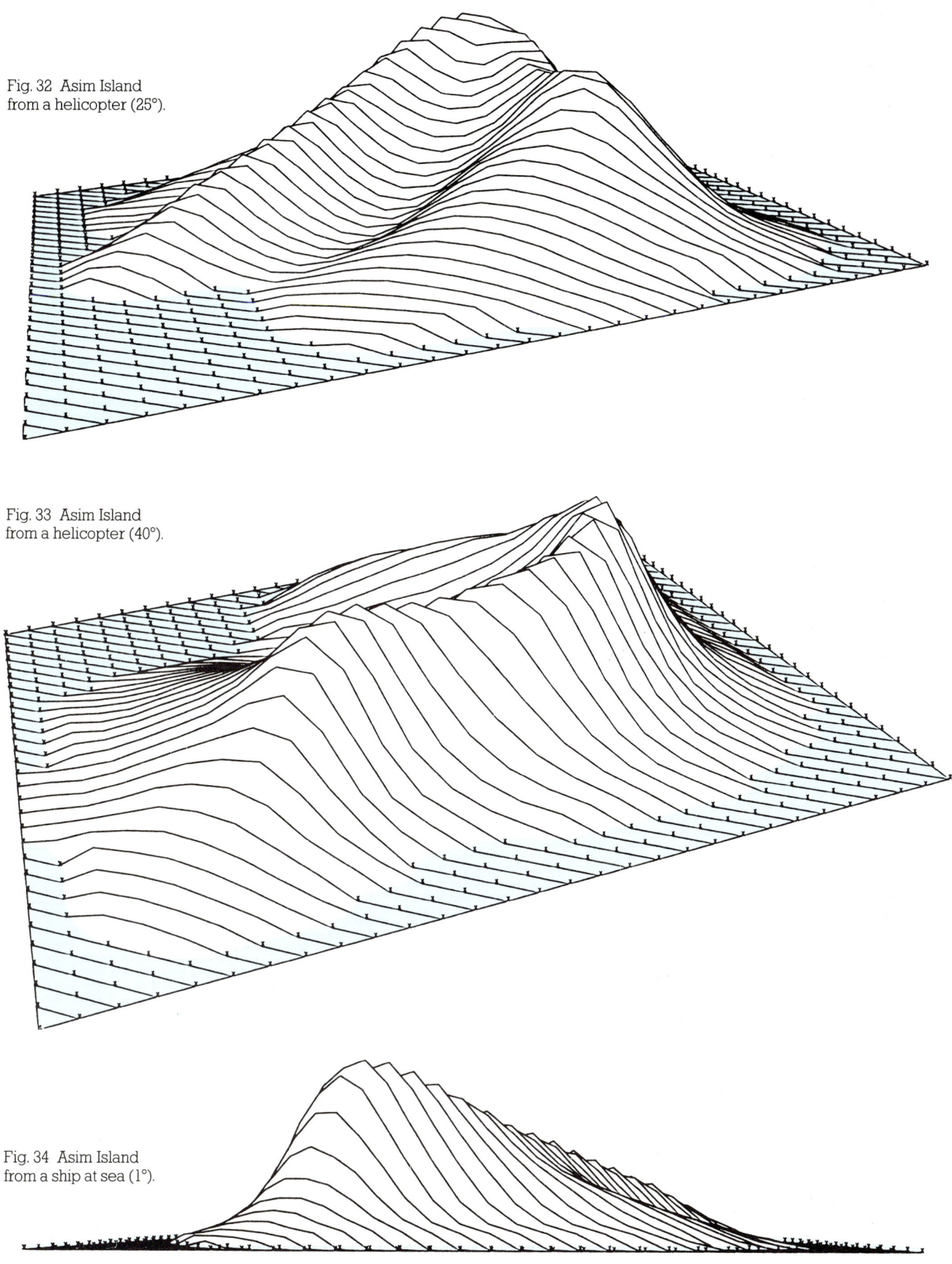

Fig. 32 Asim Island from a helicopter (25°).

Fig. 33 Asim Island from a helicopter (40°).

Fig. 34 Asim Island from a ship at sea (1°).

More contours

Some contours from part of Map Extract 11 (Sevenoaks) have been drawn on Fig. 35. The map has been turned upside-down so that it is easier to relate the diagram (Fig. 36) to the contour pattern.

1 Find the area in Fig. 35 on the map extract.
2 Trace the outline of Fig. 36. Now mark on the 100 m and 150 m contours. (Fig. 31 may help you.)
3 Trace the map (Fig. 35) and (i) shade in the area under 120 m (ii) shade in the area between 150 m and 160 m (iii) mark the highest point (iv) mark three of the steepest slopes by arrows pointing downhill.

Remember that contours are only imaginary lines. They have often been interpreted using spot heights.

4 Trace the map in Fig. 37 and mark on the spot heights. Draw the contour pattern at 50 m intervals. (A professional map-maker would be able to look at the landscape!) Hints: (i) colour all the points that are below a certain contour (in this example say 200 m) (ii) shade in another colour all the points above a certain contour (say 400 m) (iii) now study the pattern and try to draw the 200 m contour and the 400 m contour (iv) fit in the other contours.
5 Look at Map Extract 4. Can you find your pattern?

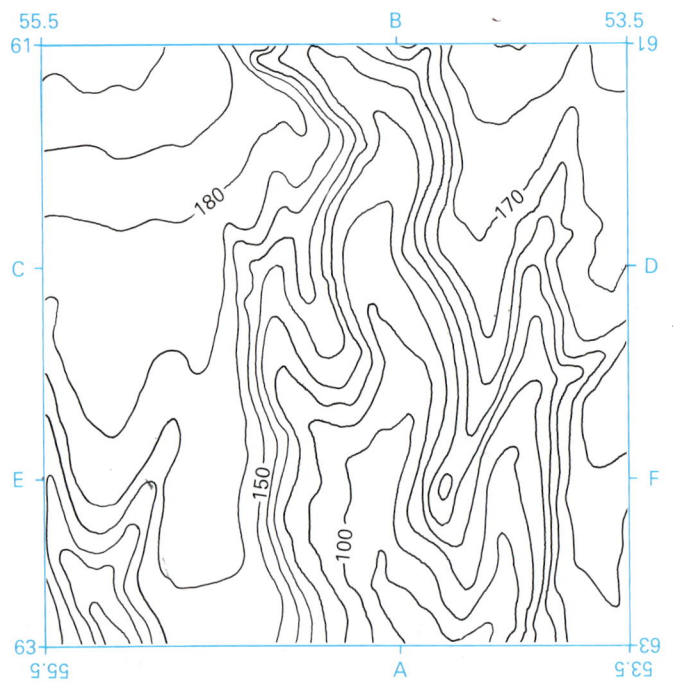

Fig. 35 North at the bottom! Scale 1:25 000.

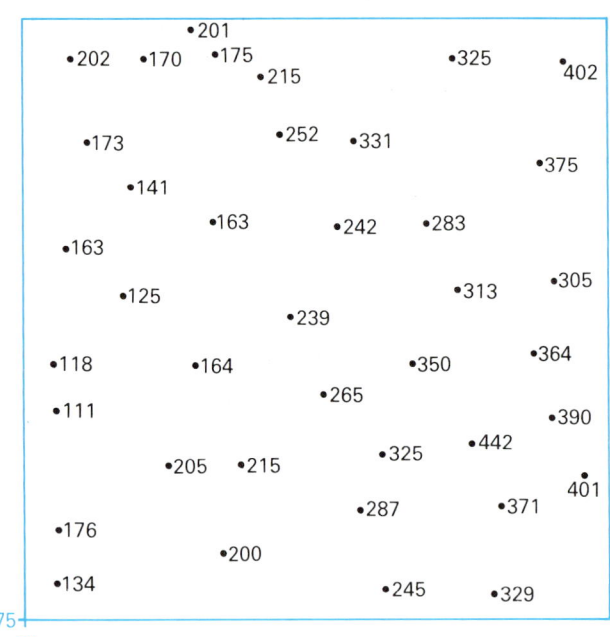

Fig. 37 Spot heights in metres for contour drawing.

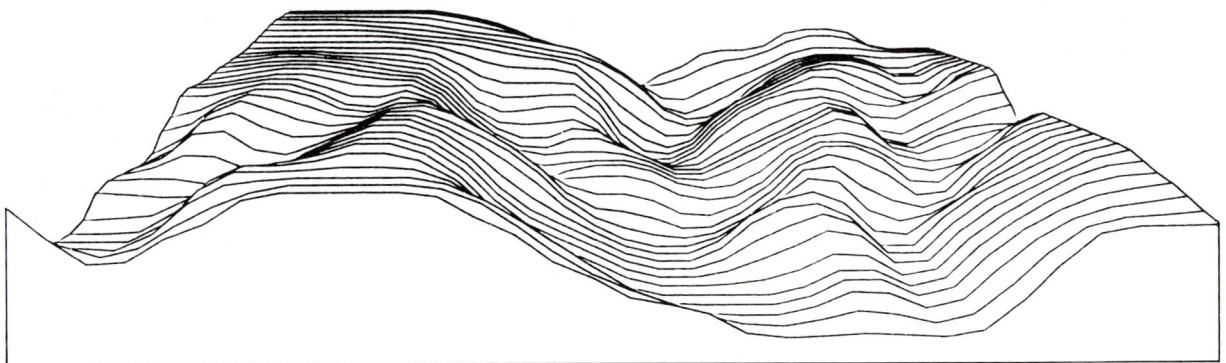

Fig. 36 Block diagram of the map on Fig. 35.

Cross-sections

What is a cross-section?

In Exercise 2 on page 18 you sliced the top off Asim Island with a horizontal cut along a contour. If instead you cut vertically across the contours, like cutting a cake, you reveal a **cross-section**. Figs. 38 and 39 show this for Asim Island.

It is very useful to be able to imagine cross-sections across a landscape. It takes practice, but once you understand contours it is possible. When you draw a section from the landscape or from a map by eye, it is called a **sketch** section.

6 Sections (i), (ii) and (iii) in Fig. 40 were taken along AB, CD and EF on the map in Fig. 35. Which section is which? Which end of each is each letter?

7 The photograph (Fig. 41) is looking south towards A in Fig. 35 (up the map in this case!). (i) Draw a sketch section across the valley from the photograph.
(ii) Draw a sketch section along the line C to B and along line B to D in Fig. 35.

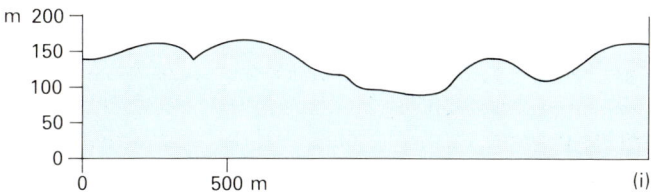
(i)

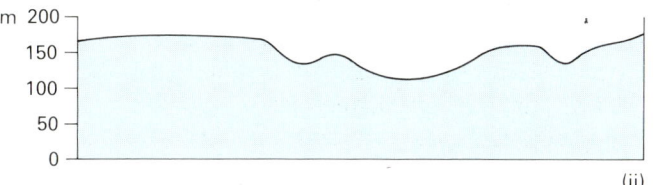
(ii)

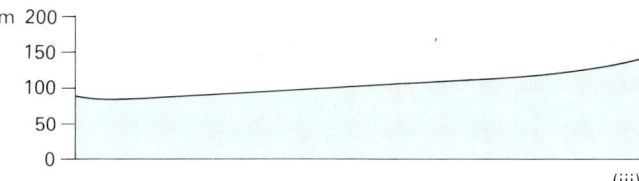
(iii)

Fig. 40 Three sections across Fig. 35.

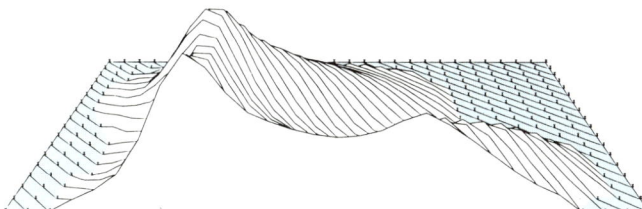

Fig. 38 Asim Island cut through.

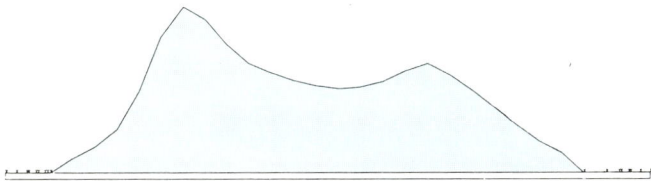

Fig. 39 Cross-section through Asim Island.

Fig. 41 Looking from the north towards 5462 on Map Extract 11.

Cross-sections from contours

Fig. 42 Lassington Hill from 807201 (Map Extracts 1 and 2).

Fig. 43 Distortion!

How to draw a cross-section

These pages explain how to draw an accurate cross-section. The example used is across the valley of the River Leadon and up the slopes of Lassington Hill, which can be seen on Map Extracts 1 and 2 (8021) and in Fig. 42. Follow each step on the diagram in Fig. 44:

1 Place the straight edge of a piece of paper on the map between A and B.
2 Mark the start and the finish of the section.
3 Make sure you know the contour interval on the map. Make a mark in each place that you cross a contour.
4 On your paper mark where you cross the tops of any hills (∧) or the bottoms of any valleys (∨). Each side of a ∧ or ∨ you will cross the same height contour (if you haven't made a mistake!). Label some of the contours with their height as you go along (see Fig. 44b). Make sure you know the height at each end of the section. Go along the line again.
5 Take your paper off the map, and draw the outline diagram for the cross-section (see Fig. 44c).
   (i) Make sure that the cross-section is exactly the same length as on the map. Label the horizontal scale; it will be the same as the map.
   (ii) Choose a vertical scale (up) and mark it on. (Fig. 44c has a vertical scale of 2 mm to 5 m.)
6 Place your piece of paper on the cross-section outline. Each time you come to a contour, mark it with a light dot on the diagram at the right height.
7 Join up the dots in a smooth line to get the cross-section. Look for clues (especially spot heights) to guide you between the contours.

The land stays between the contours from one dot to the next (or you would have crossed another contour on the map). There are no 'steps' between contours.

Draw a cross-section from A to B on Fig. 45. Use the same vertical scale as on the section for XY in Fig. 45c.

Vertical exaggeration

The block diagrams of Asim Island (pages 18 and 19) were drawn with no vertical exaggeration – the vertical scale is the same as the horizontal, and the slopes are as they are in reality. But Asim Island is very small, and the map large scale. Sections drawn across larger areas and at smaller scales show that the real world hills and valleys are small and the slopes difficult to see. Fig. 44d shows the section at 1:25 000 without vertical exaggeration. Usually sections are drawn with some vertical exaggeration – but remember that when the vertical scale is more than ten times the horizontal the impression gets very distorted (Fig. 43!). In mountainous areas no more than *five times* is sensible.

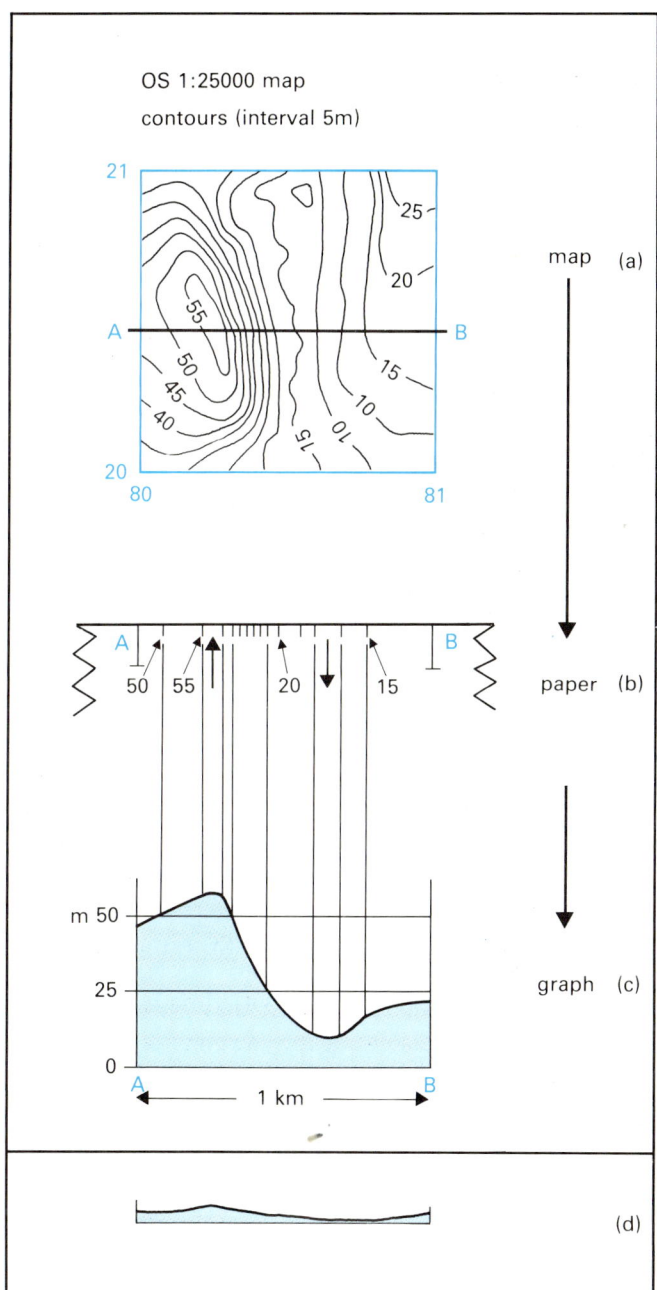

Fig. 44 Drawing cross-section AB on Map Extract 2, scale 1:25 000
(c) vertical scale × 10,
(d) no vertical exaggeration).

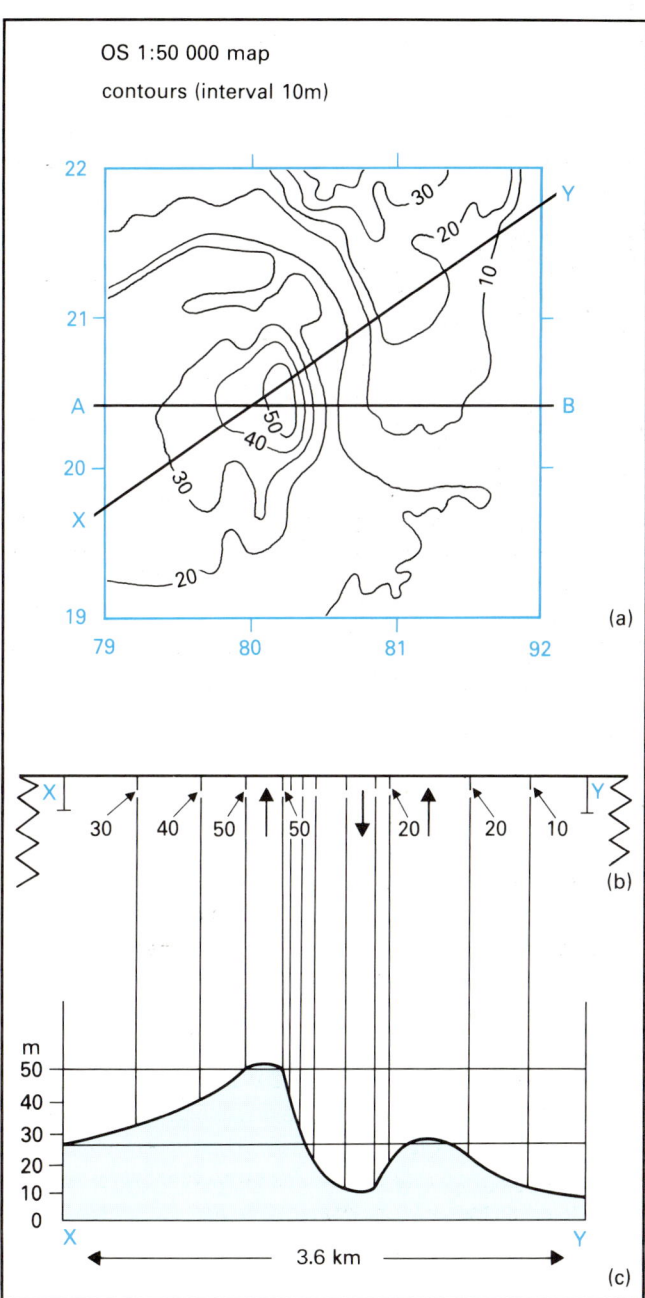

Fig. 45 Cross-section XY on Map Extract 1, scale 1:50 000
(vertical scale × 20).

Types of slope

Fig. 46 The Long Mynd. The grid lines are from Map Extract 14.

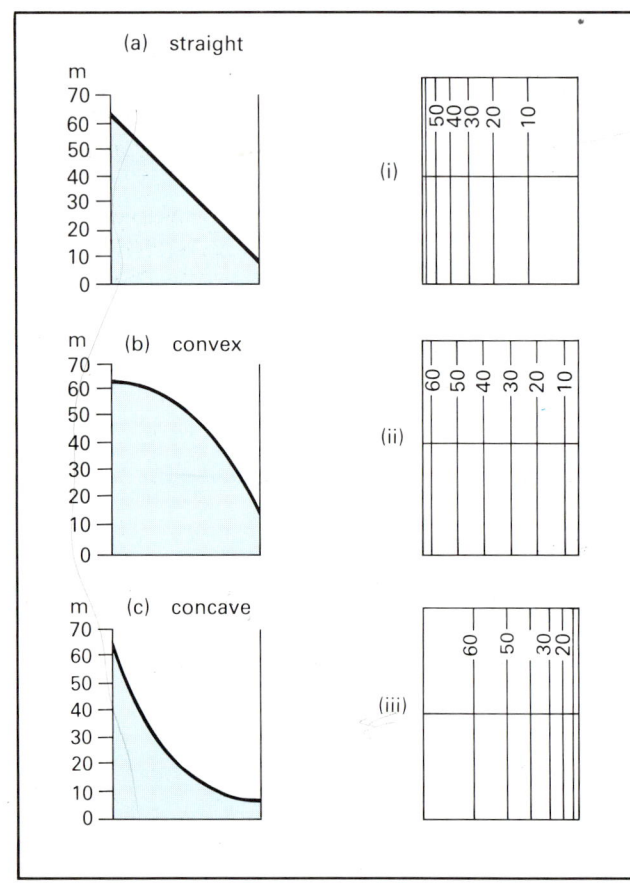

Fig. 47 Types of slope.

Slope shapes
There are three simple types of slope: (a) straight (b) convex and (c) concave. Often in Britain slopes are combinations of these.

1 In Fig. 47 the contour maps are not opposite the correct slopes. Which map goes with which slope?
2 Find three different types of slope on Fig. 46. (i) Draw a sketch section of each slope. (ii) On your sketch sections label the slopes. Are there any combinations of types? (iii) Draw a small contour pattern for each slope.
3 Look at Map Extract 11. Draw sketch sections: (i) from the crossroads at 588602 to Yeldham Manor (586888) (ii) from One Tree Hill (561531) to 565520 (iii) up the path from Woodlands (565607) to 561608.
4 Describe the slopes you would walk up or down along each section.

Gradient
Road signs warn users of steep gradients (Fig. 49).
Gradients are measured in three ways (Fig. 48): (i) A **ratio** of how far you go along in order to rise or fall one unit of height. 1 in 5 means that you go up or down 1 metre for every 5 metres you go along. (ii) A **percentage**. A 10% slope is one which for every 100 m you go along (horizontal) you go up or down 10 m (vertical). A 6% slope

is 6 m up for every 100 m along. A 1 in 5 slope is a 20% slope. (iii) An **angle** in degrees.

The gradient of a slope is always measured straight up or down the slope, e.g. across the contours at right angles. Gradients of roads or other routes just follow the route.

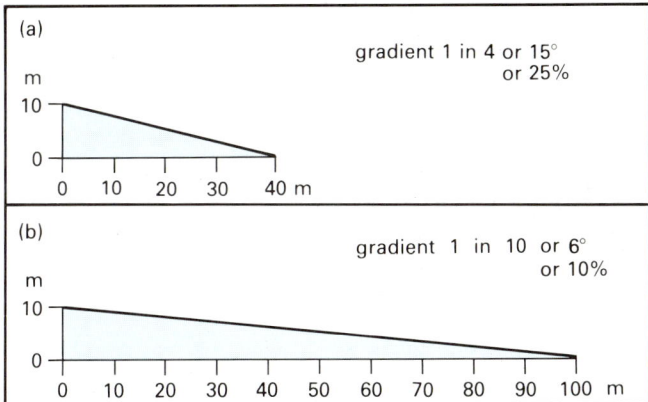

Fig. 48 Gradient measurement

Fig. 49 Wrynose-Hardknott Pass, Lake District

Gradients can be measured on the map by calculating the distance from one contour to the next. On Map Extract 3 the path from Gibbet Hill (503811) to West Blackdown (493816) crosses 14 contours downhill in 1000 m distance. The vertical interval between contours is 10 m, so the drop is 140 m. The average gradient of the path is 140 m in 1 000 m, or about 1 in 7 (14%).

5   What is the average gradient up the track from the car park at 518835 to White Hill?
6   You cycle from Peter Tavy (5177) on the upper road to Paisley (515765). What is (i) the steepest uphill (ii) the steepest downhill for you according to the map-makers' signs? Is there an easier way?

The 'gradient measurer' (Fig. 50) is for use only with 1:50 000 maps and 10 m interval contours.

7   Make a gradient measurer along the edge of a piece of card. On Map Extract 3 a new quarry is to be opened on White Tor (5478). Plan a route for a mineral railway from the quarry to the A386. The gradient must not exceed 1 in 15.
8   The stone is right, but should it be quarried?

Intervisibility

How much of the surrounding land can be seen from a viewpoint? Fig. 51 shows the 'dead land' (land that cannot be seen) for a person standing at Y.

9   If you were a look-out would you do better to stand on top of a concave or a convex slope?
10 On Map Extract 3 draw a sketch section to see if you would be able to see the top of White Tor from the river bridge to the WNW (5279).
11 You stand at the top of Pike of Stickle – Map Extract 7 (2707). You have friends at (i) Buscoe (2505) (ii) the footbridge (2706) (iii) Bow Fell (2406) and at (iv) Angle Tarn (2407). Who can you see (when they wave flags!)?

Fig. 50   Fig. 51 Contour pattern and cross-section A–B

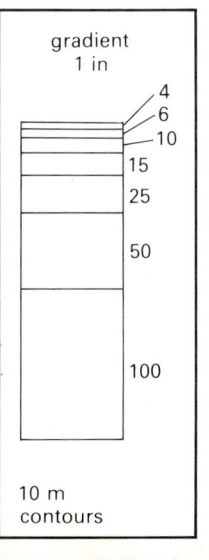

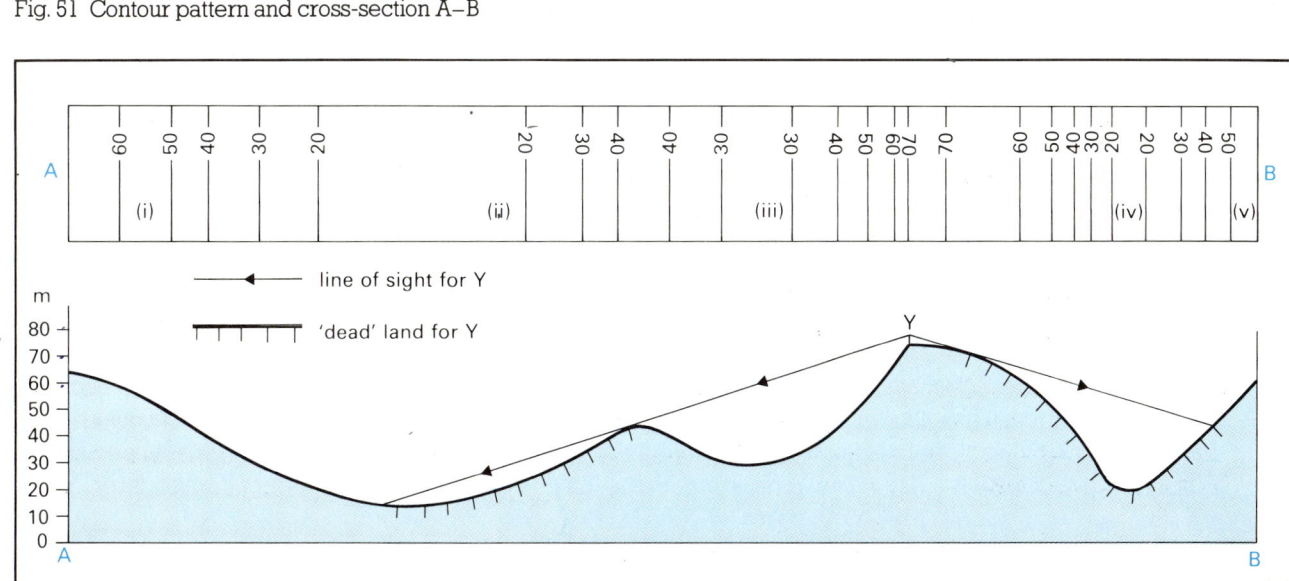

Landforms

Fig. 52 Langdale Valley, looking south-east from GR 265070, Map Extract 7.

It is important to be able to recognise landforms from their contour patterns on the map. If you are to describe the landscape to someone else you need to know the names of landforms as well.

Rivers and valleys

Rivers flow across contours at right-angles – that is straight down the slope – unless they have been channelled by man. If they have a **valley** it will show up as V-shaped knotches in the contour pattern, with the river flowing through the apex of the V. Two valleys that cut alongside each other and then join leave a **spur** between them. If a spur is flat-topped and blunt it may be called a **shoulder**. When a valley winds or zig-zags the down-cutting can form **interlocking spurs**.

When a river has cut down in a series of stages, or has changed its course, it can leave its previous valley bottom as **terraces**. Terraces can also be formed by layers of more resistant rock. When a river moves to one side of its valley undercutting it it can form **river cliffs**. The flat bottom of a river valley can be a **flood plain**. Where there is no river in a valley it is a **dry valley**. A **pass** or **gap** is a valley cutting through an area of highland.

A large flat area of land is a **plain**.

Hills and mountains

A **hill** is a general term used in uplands for features (often less than 400 m high) that are not high or rugged enough to be called **mountains**. A **knoll** is a small round hill. A **ridge** is a long narrow area of highland, which is sometimes also a spur. The **summit** of a hill or mountain is its highest point, and a **crest** can be the top line of a ridge, spur or scarp.

An **escarpment** (**scarp**) is a steep, cliff-like slope, usually marking the edge of a high flat upland (a **plateau**) or the front edge of a **cuesta**. A cuesta is a landform with a steep scarp face and a gentle **dip-slope** formed by layers of rock rising to the surface at an angle.

A **col** or **saddle** is a high gap between summits.

Landforms created by glaciation or by coastal work are mentioned on pages 37 and 38.

Each landform can be described in more detail by adding adjectives like high, low; straight, winding; steep, gentle; flat, undulating, rugged; convex, concave; symmetrical, asymmetrical; small, large, etc.

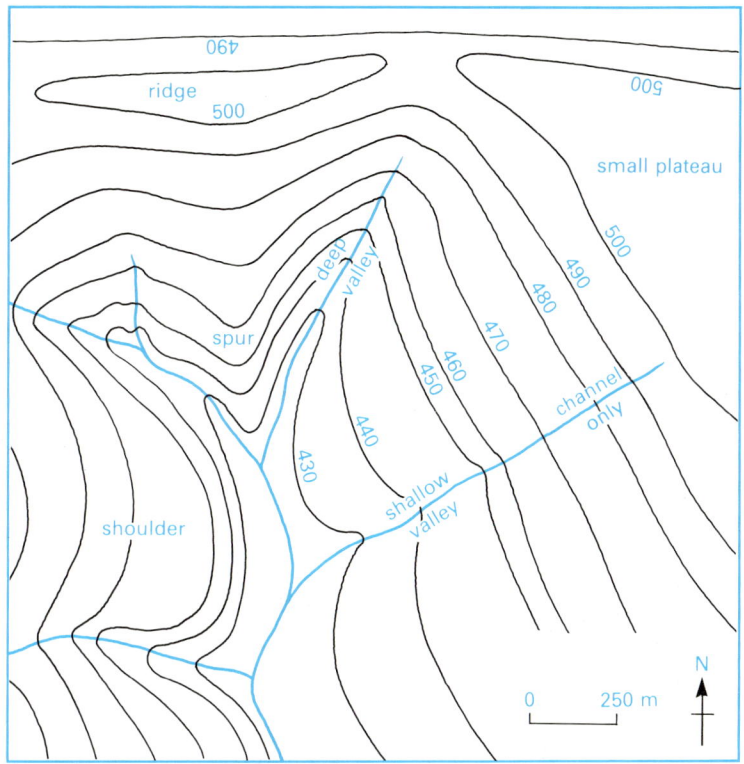

Fig. 53 Landform contour patterns.

Most of these landforms appear on photographs and maps in this book. To locate something on a photograph use the photograph reference (PR). This works like a four-figure map reference. The first two figures tell you how many centimetres to go across the photograph, the second two figures how many centimetres up. Just use a centimetre ruler. For example Fig. 52 PR 0408 means 4 cm across and 8 cm up which brings you to an area where a summit is visible.

For each landform: (i) locate it on the photograph (ii) locate it on the map extract and give a grid reference (iii) draw its contour pattern.
(Fig. 53 may help with some contour patterns)

1 Fig. 41 (a) dry valley PR 0205
  (b) dip slope PR 0405.
2 Fig. 42 (a) terrace PR 0602 hill PR 0206.
3 Fig. 46 (a) valley PR 1204 (b) shoulder PR 0604
  (c) plateau PR 0707.
4 Fig. 52 flood plain PR 1205.
5 Fig. 60 scarp PR 0501 (not on a map extract).
6 Fig. 66 (a) valley PR 0602 (b) spur PR 0701
  (c) Pass or gap PR 0407.
7 Fig. 71 (a) pass or gap PR 0907 (b) ridge PR 0508
  (c) col or saddle PR 0308.
8 Fig. 81 plain PR 1105.

Settlements

Farms and hamlets

Persh Farm is a small cluster of buildings. The farmhouse is shown in Fig. 54, and nearby there are barns and sheds (Fig. 55). The track from the farm leads to the main road into Gloucester. On Map Extract 2 (1:25 000) the farm buildings are marked at 810208, but on Map Extract 1 (1:50 000) they have become a single small symbol.

Persh Farm is a place where people live – and work as well – and can be described as a settlement.

Villages

Great Totham North (Fig. 56a) in square 8613 on Map Extract 15 is a larger settlement. It is only relatively large since it has a population of less than 200 people. Again it consists of a group of buildings where people live. Some of them work locally. There are about 60 houses and two of them are farmhouses. There is also a shop and a chapel.

It is difficult to tell what a building is used for from the map, unless like the chapel and the public house it is shown by a conventional sign. The difficulty is illustrated by the buildings around the outside of the triangle of roads making up much of Great Totham North. They are almost all bungalows for elderly people.

Two village centres are shown in Fig. 56a and b.
1 What types of building can be seen in the photo of
   (i) Great Totham North (Fig. 56a) and   (ii) Croyde (Fig. 56b)?
2 Make a list of the buildings shown by special symbols in   (i) Great Totham South (centred on 8511 on Map Extract 15, scale 1:50 000), and   (ii) Croyde (on Map Extract 10, scale 1:25 000). Which scale of map gives most information?

Fig. 54 Persh Farmhouse from the orchard at 809208 looking NNE.

Fig. 55 Persh Farm buildings from 810208 looking to the SE. Gloucester Cathedral is in the distance.

Fig. 56a Great Totham North.

Fig. 56b Croyde.

How big is a village?
It is fairly easy to pick out a farm on Map Extract 15, but how big is a village on this kind of map? Remember the word 'village' is used very loosely and is difficult to define. It is certainly not easy to tell the difference between a village and a small town on the map.

Hamlets, which are rather like very small villages, are even more difficult. However, size can be a rough guide:
  hamlets in general take up less than 0.25 km^2;
  villages fill between 0.25 km^2 and 1 km^2;
  towns are usually larger than 1 km^2.

3 On the basis of size how would you describe: (i) Great Totham South (ii) Maldon (iii) Woodham Walter on Map Extract 15?

4 Does a hamlet become a village if it has a post office and a pub?

Settlement shape

The shape and form of a settlement is often influenced by the relief and the communications around it. Many settlements are **linear** – they are built along a road, a river, a lake or seashore, a valley bottom or ridge top. Some settlements are **compact** and **nucleated** – they may be round or squarish. Some are spread out with many open spaces – a **dispersed** settlement which may look more like individual homesteads or several small hamlets (Tiptree Heath at 8815 on Map Extract 15 is an example).

Many settlements are combinations of these patterns, often with a compact centre and linear 'arms' stretching away along roads.

5 On Map Extract 13 study the settlements of Tebay, Orton, Raisbeck and Longdale. Decide (i) what kind of settlement each is (ii) what shape and form each has.

Towns

A settlement is a place where people live and always includes buildings used as homes. But the larger a settlement is the more buildings are used for work, leisure and services.

Fig. 57 shows part of the busy city of Gloucester. The cathedral is on Map Extracts 1 and 2, in square 8318.

1 Put a piece of tracing paper over Fig. 57. Mark on the frame and the cathedral. (Its shadow should tell you the time of day and the season!)
2 In your margins mark on a north arrow and a scale line.
3 Trace on   (i) the railway   (ii) roads.
4 Shade in areas that you can see are houses and gardens.
5 Shade in open spaces. Decide what each space is used for.
6 Compare your map carefully with the 1:25 000 map. The corners of the photograph are at approximately 830187, 830192, 835187, and 835192. Does your pattern match?
7 Mark on any more buildings whose use you can see or work out from the photograph or map.

Your work with the photograph and the map will have given you some idea of the **function** of part of Gloucester – that is 'what it does'.

Special maps of land use and of urban function can be drawn after fieldwork, and really it is necessary to visit a place to study its function. OS maps give some facts and many clues, but by themselves are not enough.

Fig. 57 Vertical air photograph of Gloucester.

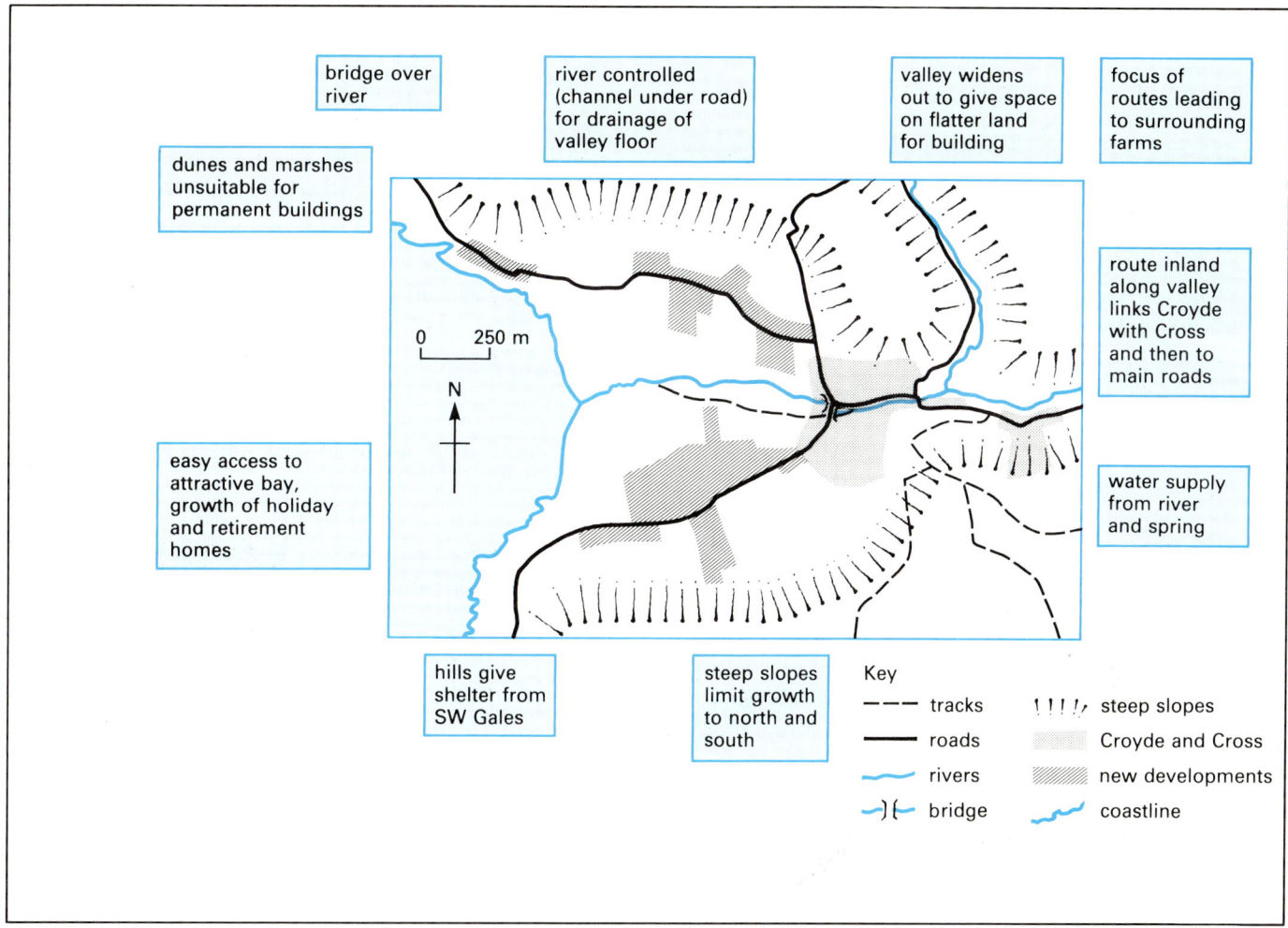

Fig. 58 The site of the village of Croyde.

Location: situation and site

The **situation** of a settlement is its position in relation to the surrounding landscape, communications and other settlements.

The **site** of a settlement is more local – its position in relation to local relief, water supply, farmland, and economic activities like mining.

It is difficult to untangle site and situation, and usually it is sensible to study both together to answer the questions 'Why is a settlement where it is?' and 'What has helped it to survive and grow?'.

Fig. 58 is an annotated sketch map of the site of Croyde. Fig. 56b is a photograph of its centre, and it is on Map Extracts 9 and 10. Croyde is in North Devon, about half a kilometre from the sea, in a valley that provides a routeway to link the coastal road with inland settlements and main roads.

8 Put a piece of tracing paper over Fig. 58. Draw the frame of the map and the frames of the annotations. Use the sketch map and Map Extract 10 and with a ruler draw a line from each 'annotation box' to the places on the map to which it refers.

When studying the site of a settlement think about each of the following questions:

(i) Relief – look at the contours – is the settlement built on a flat plain, a hilltop, a terrace above a plain, sloping land (steep or gentle?), in a valley?

(ii) Water supply and drainage – is the settlement by a river, on a stream, next to a spring, by a lake, on a coast?

(iii) Shelter – is it sheltered by hills, in a bay, on an inlet, in a valley?

(iv) Communications – is the settlement at a bridging or crossing point, on a main road, at a junction of roads, has it a railway station, a harbour or port, a canal?

(v) Are there any other special things about the site?

9 Describe the site and situation of Appledore in square 4630 on Map Extract 9.

10 Use Map Extract 13 to draw an annotated sketch map of the site and situation of Tebay and Old Tebay.

11 Choose a site for a new village on: (i) Map Extract 10 (ii) Map Extract 3. Explain your choices.

Communications

OS maps give detailed information about roads, paths and railways.

1. Study the Key Sheet to the 1:50 000 maps (Map Extract 5). List all the things you can find out about a road from these maps.
2. Look at Map Extract 13. You go from Holme House (6506) to Tebay via Raisbeck (6407) and Gaisgill (6305). Describe each of the different kinds of road on which you would travel.

Gradient (see page 25), possible flooding, and exposure to bad weather conditions are important considerations when routes are established.

3. Why do motorways and main roads avoid steep gradients as much as possible?
4. Look at Map Extract 13. (i) What physical feature do the A685 and the M6 follow? (ii) What special construction-works help to keep the roads level? (Give GRs to support your map evidence.) (iii) How does the design of the M6 avoid the danger of flooding near Tebay? (iv) Why has the road in Fig. 59 crossed the highland at 6809?

Industry

There is some evidence on OS maps of what industrial activity is taking place, but the amount of evidence mainly depends on the type of industry.

Extractive industry

Mines, quarries and pits are usually clearly marked. In the UK on lowlands the **mines** are usually for coal (some are named 'Collieries') or in a few cases for salt. On high limestone areas mines are often disused zinc/lead mines, and in areas with igneous rocks can be copper or tin mines.

Quarries may be for open-cast coal or iron ore, or for roadstone in granite, limestone or ancient hard rocks. They may also be for slate, for chemicals in limestones, or for chalk and limestone used especially for cement-making. You need evidence of the rock type before you can tell what is quarried.

Pits are usually for sand, gravel or clay. The sand is sometimes used to make glass, but most sand and gravel is used to make concrete. The clay is usually for brick-making, but in granite areas of SW England it will be china clay for the pottery industry.

5. What extractive industry is there in the area of Map Extract 6? Give GRs to support your evidence.

Manufacturing industry

Sometimes an activity is named (e.g. Brick Works, Chemical Works) but often a large building is marked on the map and just labelled 'Works (Wks)' or 'Mill'. Other factories, factory estates and warehouses are usually marked but not labelled. You can recognise them because they are (i) large patches of building, but (ii) not cut up by roads like housing estates are, and (iii) usually close to a main road or railway line.

Look at Map Extract 6

6. How many labelled 'Works' can you find?
7. What other areas do you think are mainly factories and warehouses?
8. Choose two areas that you think are mainly factories and draw a sketch map of each to show its transport links.
9. What other 'lines' on the map are important for industry besides roads, rail and water?

Tertiary or service industry

Unless a building is named (e.g. 'School') it is difficult to recognise service industry on an OS map. The identification of shops and offices really needs local fieldwork or special large-scale plans.

Fig. 59 Filming a Volvo advertisement. On Map Extract 13 looking ESE from 685095.

Fig. 60 An old lead mine, smelter and flue, in Swaledale, North Yorkshire.

Evidence of the past

One very good source of information about the past is old maps (see page 45), but OS maps do include some information about past activities. Some of this information is specially selected, like sites of battles, but most of it is selected to explain features that are still visible on the landscape. Thus disused mines (Fig. 60) and quarries, routes of dismantled railways (Fig. 42), sites of deserted villages, and 'antiquities' are all marked.

10 Look at Map Extract 3. In the SE corner (east of easting 51 and south of northing 79) there are ten **different** kinds of 'antiquity' marked.
   List the ten different antiquities. Find out what each one is, when it was probably constructed, and say what you would expect to see at each site.

Describing landscape

A large area
Now that you have fully learned to read a map you should be able to describe the landscape in detail. All the time you should use grid references, distances, directions and area measurements in your descriptions.

1 Describe the relief and drainage of the land in Map Extract 11.
   (i) Are there major divisions of the area (e.g. into highland, lowland, flat land, undulating land)?
   (ii) What major relief features are there (e.g. scarps, spurs, ridges, valleys, plateaux, plains)? Give compass directions for the main features (e.g. N–S valleys).
   (iii) Describe the drainage (the river pattern).
   (iv) Are there major areas of particular vegetation?
2 Describe the settlement and communication pattern of the area on Map Extract 11.
   (i) What large settlements are there? Where are they located?
   (ii) Is there a particular pattern to the distribution of settlements (e.g. in valleys)?
   (iii) Describe the communication pattern and the way it matches the relief and drainage and the settlement pattern.
   (iv) Are there areas that are put to special uses (e.g. mining, National Trust)?

Describing a small area
Follow the same sequence, but look for every detail!
3 Describe the landscape (everything) in square 6405 on Map Extract 13.

Map interpretation

The first part of this book has developed the basic skills of map reading. From here on the emphasis is on the interpretation of what you read on maps – what can be found out from the information.

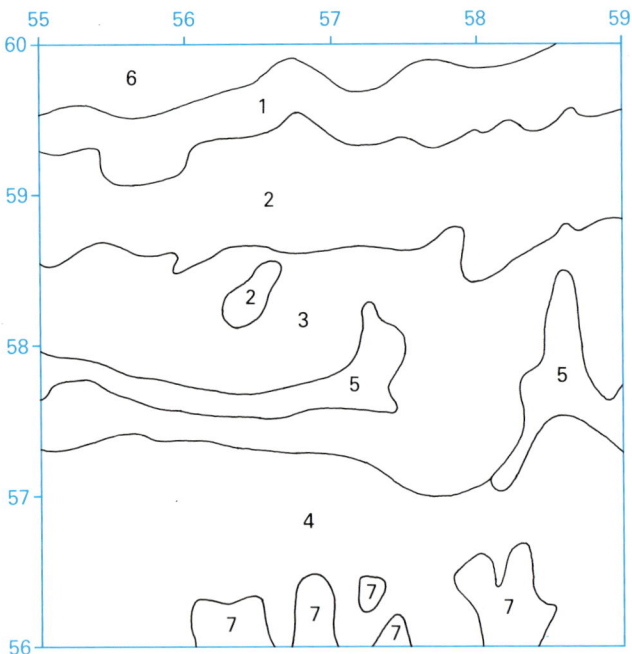

Key
Solid geology
1 Upper and Middle Chalk (white)
2 Lower Chalk (marly)
3 Gault Clay
4 Lower Greensand
 (sands and sandstone)

Drift geology
5 Alluvium
6 Clay and Flints
7 Head
 (clay, sand and stones)

Fig. 61 Surface geology, part of Map Extract 11

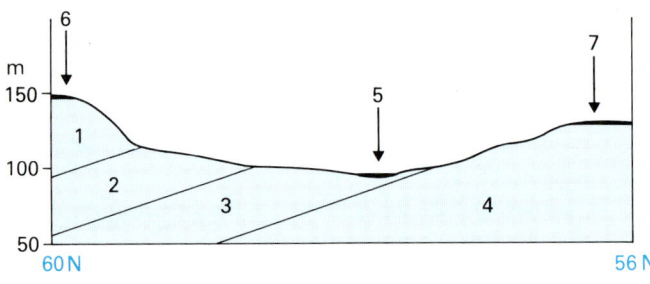

Fig. 62 Cross-section down easting 57, Map Extract 11. Vertical exaggeration × 5, actual dip 5°.

Rock types

OS maps give a lot of clues about the **geology** of an area. You can never be certain what the rocks are at the surface without visiting it, but different rock types and different geological structures (folds, faults, tilting, etc.) do tend to produce certain types of scenery.

There are five main groups of evidence to look for:
1 Landforms – scarps, hills, plains.
2 Drainage – surface water, river patterns.
3 Detailed topography – rock outcrops etc.
4 Vegetation.
5 Human activities – quarries, farming etc.

Working with the aid of simple geology maps develops the skill of looking for evidence. The maps (Figs. 61 and 63) show outcrops of **solid** rocks at the surface and also the more recent deposits (**drift**).

1 Trace the surface geology from Fig. 61. Put your tracing over the 16 squares of Map Extract 11. Does the pattern of geology match the relief pattern?
2 Take each rock type in turn. Use the five headings above to make a list of the kind of scenery each has. (Figs. 35, 36 and 41 are of the chalk.)
3 Look at the cross-section Fig. 62 (see Fig. 92 for another diagram). How has the dip (tilt) of the layers of rock helped to create this scenery?
4 Draw N–S cross-sections like Fig. 62 to show what you think the scenery would be like if (i) the rocks dipped in the opposite direction (down to the south) (ii) if the rocks were in horizontal layers.
5 Do Exercises 1 and 2 for Fig. 63, Map Extract 3.
6 Draw a cross-section along grid line northing 85, from easting 50 to easting 56. (i) Mark on the surface geology. (ii) Try to show the underground geology (like Fig. 62). Remember that the granite and dolerite pushed up into the other solid rock.
7 Read the description of the geology of Map Extract 13 (Fig. 64) and study the map. Write a list of as many differences as you can between the limestone area and the slate/shale area.
8 In a report to a camping club, explain what you think are (i) the good things (ii) the bad things about camping on each area. Which would you choose?
9 Study the area in and around the following grid squares on Map Extract 14. What rocks would you expect to find in each (give your reasons): (i) 4192 (ii) 4688 (iii) 3992 (iv) 3988 (v) 4684?

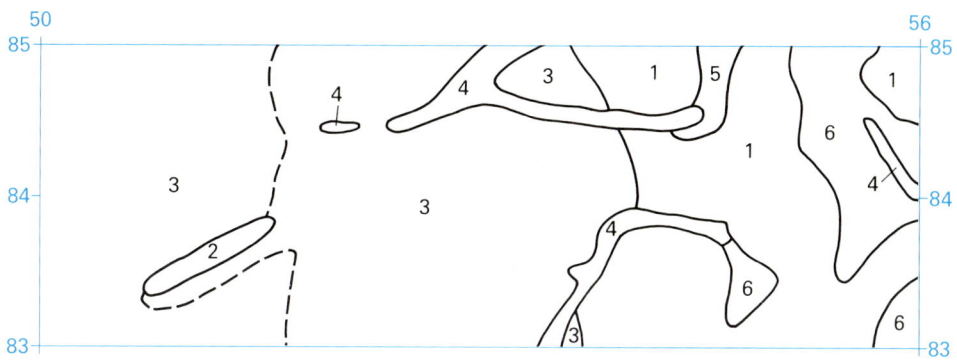

Key

Solid geology

1 Granite

2 Dolerite (hard, black volcanic rock)

3 Grits, Slates and Limestones

— — — Boundary of rocks changed by heat and pressure from granite

Drift geology

4 Alluvium

5 Head

6 Hill Peat (on top of granite)

Fig. 63 Surface geology, part of Map Extract 3.

> The valley floor of the River Lune is alluvium.
> To the north of the valley the rocks are massive Carboniferous Limestone.
> To the south of the valley are Silurian Slates and Shales.

Fig. 64 Map Extract 13, Tebay, surface geology.

> **Limestone** – lack of surface water, dry valleys, rock outcrops, scarps, disappearing rivers, potholes, cliffs, rough pasture, quarries.
> **Chalk** – lack of surface water, dry valleys, smooth slopes, quarries.
> **Sandstones** – (depend on strength of 'cement') rock outcrops, coniferous forests, can be moorland (e.g. Millstone Grit), scarps (e.g. Lower Greensand) or hills (e.g. Old Red Sandstone).
> **Sandy beds** – heathland, coniferous forests, sand-pits.
> **Granites** – tors, heath, bogs, peat, surface water, uplands, quarries.
> **Clay** – flat land, many streams, pools, marshes, lakes, often drainage ditches, clay-pits.
> **Alluvium** – along valley floors, often drained.
> **Sands and gravels** – flat, sometimes terraces, sand and gravel pits, often surface water.
> **Slate** – highland, rounded, quarries.
> **Ancient resistant rocks** – highlands, rock outcrops, moorland, quarries.

Fig. 65 Clues to rocks – but they are only clues!

Drainage basins and rivers

Long profiles

If you follow a river from source to mouth, you follow its 'long profile'. You can draw the profile using the same method as you use for cross-sections (see page 22) except that you follow the river with your piece of paper. You have probably seen a 'model' of a river profile like Fig. 67.

Work in groups on the following tasks:
1. Draw the long profile of (i) Map Extract 16, Afon Pennant 086325 to 110357 (ii) Extract 7, Stake Beck 273079 to its confluence with Langstack Beck (iii) Extract 13, the river from Birkgill Moss 664021 to 660049 and (iv) on Extract 3, the river from Willsworth Artillery Range 544838 to its confluence with the River Tavy. (For (i) and (ii) use a vertical scale of 2 cm to 50 m, for (iii) and (iv) use 1 cm to 50 m.)
2. Are the profiles like the model?
3. Can you explain any of the slope changes?
4. Choose a place on each river where (i) the profile is steep and (ii) gentle. Draw a sketch section across the valley at each place.
5. Is there a relationship between the long profiles and the cross-sections in these four examples?

Watersheds

A watershed is a line dividing water that drains into one river from water that drains into another. Watersheds follow the tops of hills, ridges and spurs. (Pages 52–56 have more work on this topic.)

Look at Map Extract 16. Fig. 68 shows the main rivers and some of the major watersheds.

6. Put a piece of tracing paper on Extract 16 and transfer the information on Fig. 68 to it. Now draw in the watersheds separating: (i) rivers A and B (ii) rivers B and D.
7. Why is the channel at (a) likely to be man-made?
8. On your completed tracing mark draw in northing 36. On the area south of this line (i) mark in all the sources of rivers and all the springs. (ii) draw in the contours at 400 m, 305 m, and 200 m. (iii) How many sources and springs are there (a) above 400 m (b) 305 to 400 m (c) 200 to 305 m (d) below 200 m? (iv) mark an arrow on each spring to show in which direction it flows. At what height are most found?

Fig. 66 Browney Gill. Looking south from 265058 on Map Extract 7.

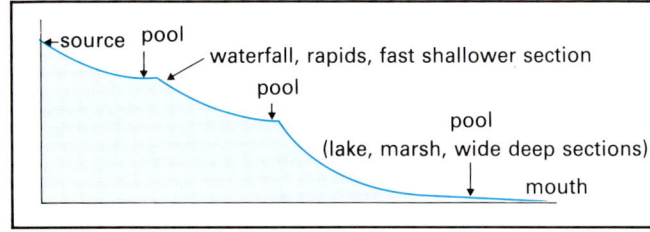

Fig. 67 'Model' of a long profile.

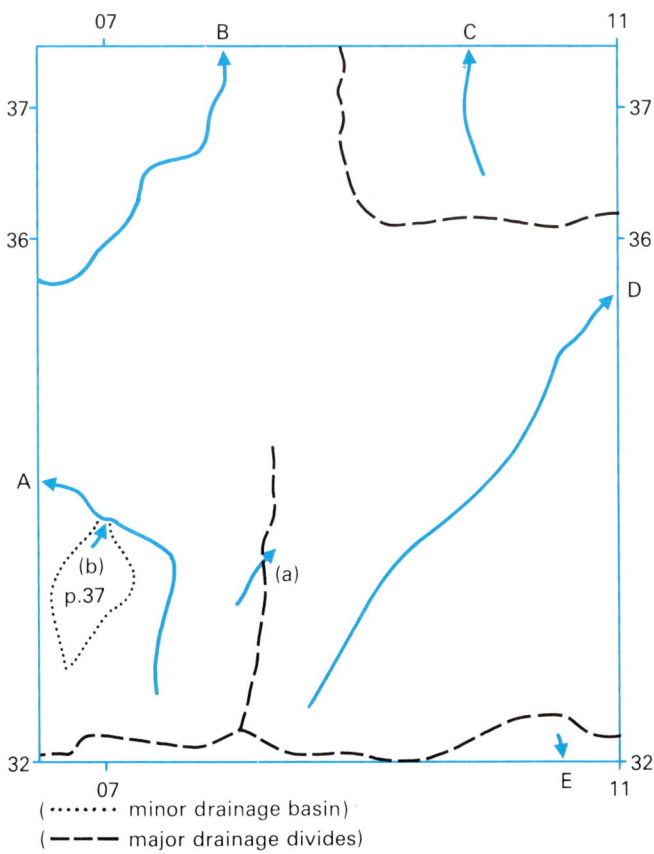

Fig. 68 Some major watersheds on Map Extract 16.

Drainage basins

Large drainage basins (e.g. the Thames) are made up of hundreds of smaller basins. On maps of the size and scale we are using we can see the whole basin of only very small streams. One is marked (b) on Fig. 68.

9 Look at Map Extract 13. Trace the river from Birkgill Moss (6602) and all its tributaries down to 660049. Use the contour information to mark on the watershed around this small drainage basin.

River patterns

The patterns rivers make are closely related to the pattern of the rocks, and in much of the UK to relief features left by glaciation (page 38).

10 Trace only the rivers in: (i) Map Extract 7, squares 2408, 2409, 2508, 2509 (ii) Extract 14, squares 4590, 4690, 4591, 4691 (iii) Extract 16, squares 0933, 1033, 0934, 1034 (iv) Extract 15, squares 8511, 8611, 8512, 8612. (Save your maps for later work.)

11 In what ways are the patterns different? Suggest possible reasons for the differences.

Drainage density

Drainage density is the length of river per square kilometre. The density depends mainly on rainfall, temperature, rock type and human activity.

12 Work out the drainage density for each of the four areas you traced for Exercise 10. Measure the approximate total length of the rivers in km, divide by the area (4 km^2), answer in km/km^2.

13 Compare (i) with (ii) and (iii) with (iv). Look at an atlas map showing rainfall in England and Wales and see if it explains any differences.

14 What effect has the scale of the map on the apparent drainage density? Why is this?

15 Look at Map Extract 13. What effect do different rock types have on drainage densities in the area (see page 34)?

River control

Nearly every large river in the UK has been straightened, its banks strengthened, its water used and its flow controlled.

16 Look at Map Extract 2 and Fig. 69. Draw a sketch map (see Fig. 70) of squares 8017, 8117, 8018, 8118. Mark on the River Severn, drainage channels, the edge of the flood plain and any terraces, and evidence of human activity to control the river.

17 Look at Map Extract 15. Draw a sketch map of the squares 8008, 8108, 8208, 8308 (valley of the River Chelmer) and annotate your map to show all the changes and uses made by people. Suggest reasons.

Fig. 69 The River Severn flood plain, looking NW from 803185 on Map Extract 2. The light coloured field is barley – not water!

1 Decide on a scale. This will depend on how big an area you are going to map. Choose a scale that makes it easy to compare with the OS map (e.g. a half or a quarter of the OS scale, or twice or four times the scale).
2 Draw a frame, label the boundary grid lines.
3 If the sketch map covers a large area lightly draw in some grid lines to guide you.
4 Choose some important line features (rivers, main roads) and draw these on as background information.
5 Mark on the built-up area of any important settlements.
6 Decide what features are important for the particular sketch map you are drawing (e.g. they are listed in Exercise 16 for the study of the flood plain area).
7 Draw the outline of the chosen features, and symbols for special features. Leave shading until last.
8 Add any annotation you need (e.g. labels, extra description, explanations, relationships etc. – see Figs. 58 and 107 for examples).
9 Make sure your key is complete, and that you have a scale, a north arrow and a title.

These are only guidelines – not rules!

Fig. 70 Drawing a sketch map from an OS map.

Glaciated landscapes

Fig. 71 Langdale Valley, looking north from 266059 on Map Extract 7.

Fig. 72 shows some of the common features found in mountains that have been glaciated. The U-shaped valley may be flooded to form a ribbon lake.

1. Put a piece of tracing paper over the photograph of Langdale (Fig. 71) and draw the outline of the main features (sky-line, valley sides, etc.).
2. The photograph was taken at 266059 on Map Extract 7. On your tracing mark and label: (i) Stake Gill (ii) Troughton Beck (iii) Rossett Gill (iv) Mart Crag (v) Black Crags (vi) Rossett Crag (vii) the footpaths.
3. On a second tracing mark and label: (i) a U-shaped valley (ii) a scree slope (iii) an alluvial fan (iv) a hanging valley (v) some irregular small hills deposited by water and melting ice.
4. Find as many other features of glaciation (see Fig. 72) as you can on Map Extract 7. Study the contour pattern for each feature.
5. Draw a full page map of an imaginary glaciated mountainous area, using contours at 100 m intervals. The highest peaks should be 1000 m. Make sure you have at least a U-shaped valley, an arête, a cirque, and a hanging valley on your map.
6. What glacial features are shown on Fig. 73?

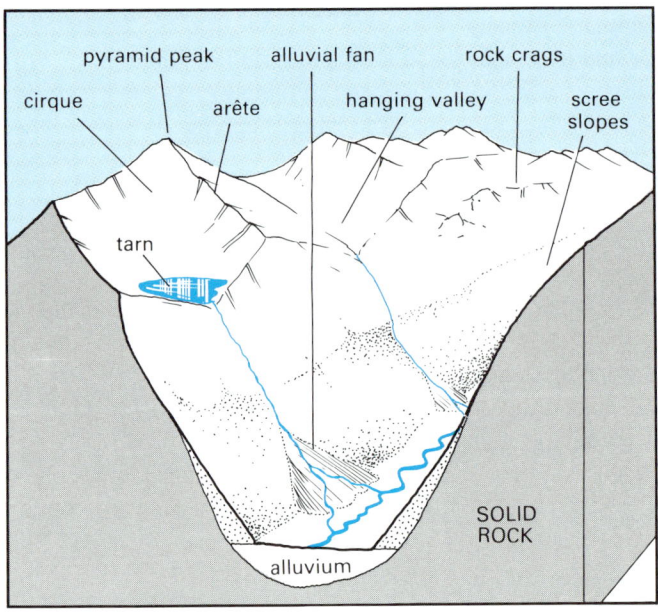

Fig. 72 A glaciated valley.

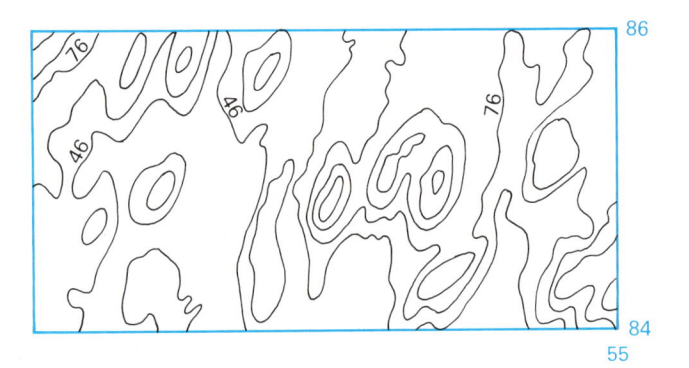

Fig. 73 Contours from OS 1:50 000 sheet 97.

Coastal landforms

The processes of **erosion** and **deposition** are most obvious and active on ocean coastlines. OS maps provide a lot of detail about coastal features.

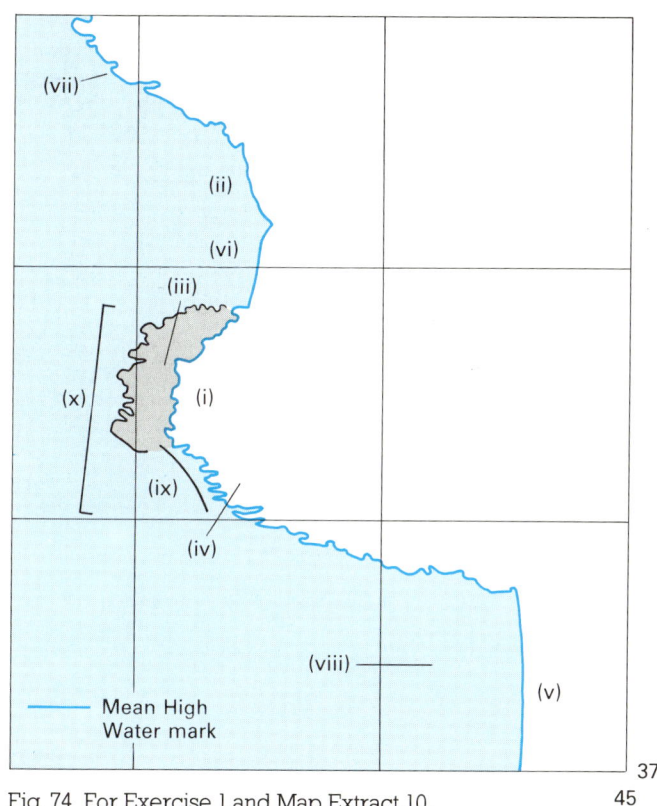

Fig. 74 For Exercise 1 and Map Extract 10.

Fig. 75 Low tide, Map Extract 10 (GR 4338).

1. Use Fig. 74 and Map Extract 10 to answer the following questions:
   What coastal features are (i) and (ii)? Is erosion or deposition the main activity on each?
   What result of coastal erosion is at (iii)? (The photograph in Fig. 75 was taken in square 4338.)
   What is the height of the cliff at (iv)?
   Where does the sand come from, and how is it brought, to form the dunes at (v)?
   What happens to the water from the river at low tide at (vi)?
   What is the distance between high and low tide at (vii) and at (viii)?
   What is (ix)? How was it formed?
2. How long would it take you to walk along the coastal path from south to north on Map Extract 2?
3. Choose a place (give its GR) for (i) swimming (ii) a cliff-top picnic (iii) collecting shell fish at low tide. Explain your choices.
4. Describe the coast at (x). Refer to cliff height, steepness, features between LWM and HWM, land just inland, etc.

Look at Map Extract 9. The 1:50 000 map gives less coastal information than the 1:25 000 map, but is still very useful. (Page 59 has more information.)

5. Draw or trace the outline of the Taw Estuary from Map Extract 9 between eastings 43 and 49, and northings 30 and 35.
6. Mark on the main coastal features. Label and annotate your map to show the way in which they are formed. Your map should include sandbanks, dunes, drained marshes, a spit, tidal marshes, a storm beach and pebble areas protecting spits from erosion.

Games and puzzles

Improve your visual and spatial perception by practice with map search, speed and accuracy.

You can make up similar games and puzzles of your own for use with other maps.

90-second speed challenge

(Use any OS 1:50 000 map extract.)

With your partner see who can locate the most:
 (i) farmhouses in 90 seconds;
 (ii) Crossroads in 90 seconds;
 (iii) river confluences in 90 seconds;
 (iv) bridges in 90 seconds;
 (v) hill tops enclosed by a contour in 90 seconds;
 (vi) 'free choice' optional in 90 seconds.

You must record each location by a four-figure grid reference so that you can check each other's scores. Highest total for the six rounds wins.

Accuracy

(Use any nine grid squares (3 × 3) on any OS 1:50 000 map extract.)

Find **all** the items listed (i) to (v) above in the nine grid squares.

Record your findings as six-figure grid references, or on tracing paper laid over the map. Highest total wins.

Map search

(Use Map Extract 14 and Fig. 76.)

The patterns in Fig. 76 can be found in grid squares on Map Extract 14: (i) three river patterns (a), (b) and (c) (ii) roads (iii) contours (iv) buildings (v) letters and numbers.

Find the squares and give a four-figure grid reference for each. Trace the square and try it on the map if you are uncertain or need help.

The winner can be the first to complete a column, or the first to find all the squares.

Make up a puzzle like this on another map extract for your partner.

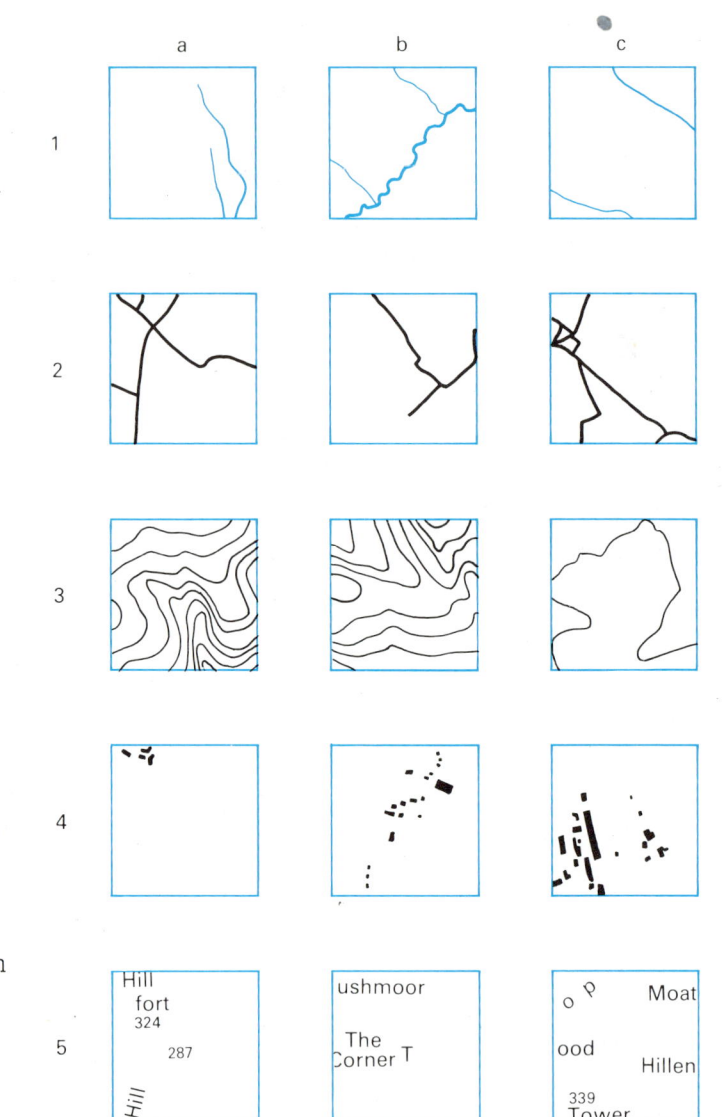

Fig. 76 Map search.

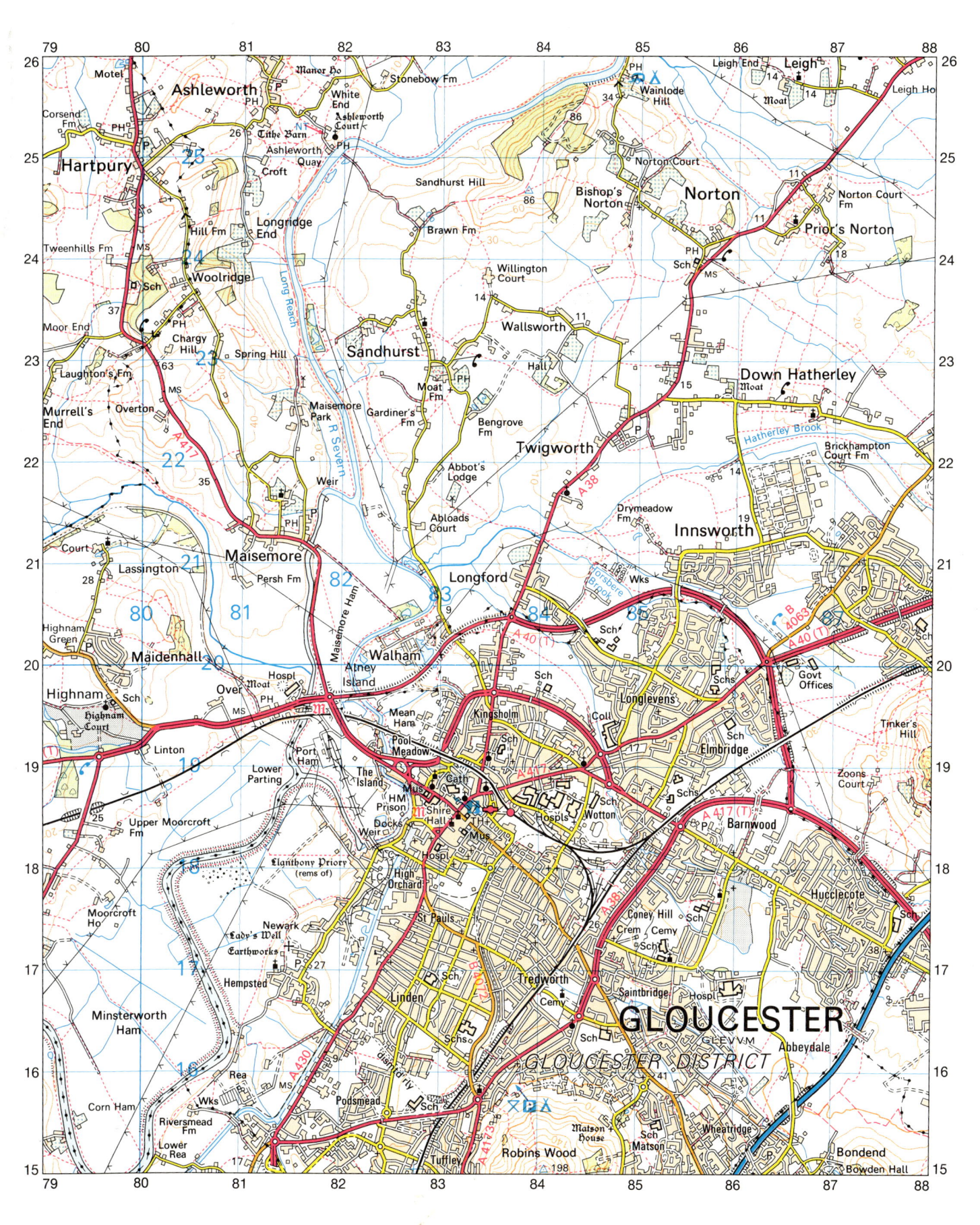

Map Extract 1

Gloucester   Sheet 162   1:50 000 Second Series

Map Extract 2

Gloucester   SO 81/91   82/92   1:25 000

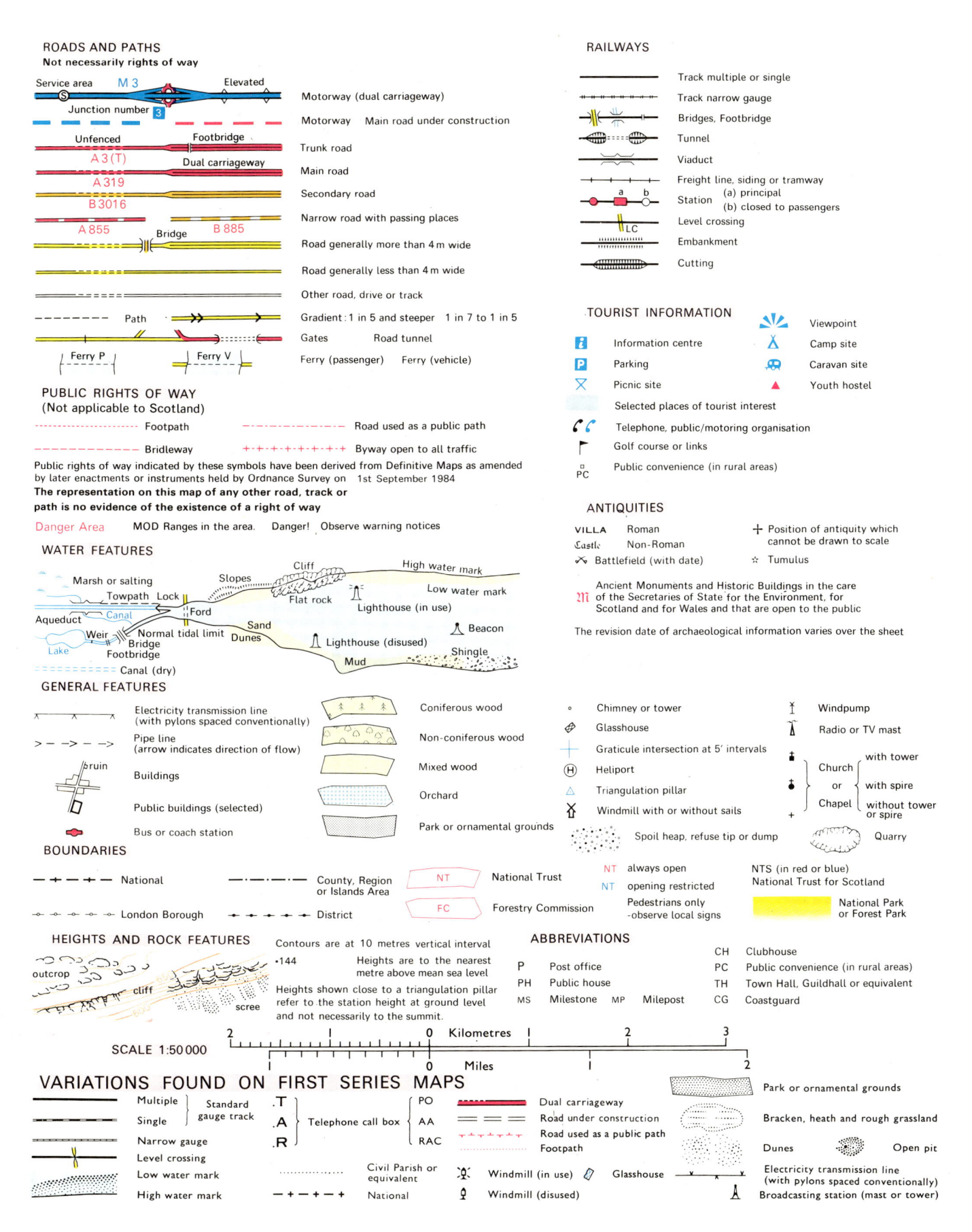

Map Extract 5

ROADS AND PATHS
Not necessarily rights of way

- Motorway (dual carriageway) — Service area, M 3, Elevated, Junction number 3
- Motorway Main road under construction
- Trunk road — Unfenced, Footbridge, A 3(T), Dual carriageway
- Main road — A 319
- Secondary road — B 3016
- Narrow road with passing places — A 855, Bridge, B 885
- Road generally more than 4 m wide
- Road generally less than 4 m wide
- Other road, drive or track
- Path
- Gradient: 1 in 5 and steeper, 1 in 7 to 1 in 5
- Gates, Road tunnel
- Ferry P, Ferry V, Ferry (passenger), Ferry (vehicle)

PUBLIC RIGHTS OF WAY
(Not applicable to Scotland)

- Footpath
- Road used as a public path
- Bridleway
- Byway open to all traffic

Public rights of way indicated by these symbols have been derived from Definitive Maps as amended by later enactments or instruments held by Ordnance Survey on 1st September 1984. The representation on this map of any other road, track or path is no evidence of the existence of a right of way

Danger Area MOD Ranges in the area. Danger! Observe warning notices

WATER FEATURES

Marsh or salting, Slopes, Cliff, High water mark, Low water mark, Towpath, Lock, Flat rock, Lighthouse (in use), Aqueduct, Canal, Ford, Sand, Beacon, Weir, Normal tidal limit, Dunes, Lighthouse (disused), Lake, Bridge Footbridge, Mud, Shingle, Canal (dry)

GENERAL FEATURES

- Electricity transmission line (with pylons spaced conventionally)
- Pipe line (arrow indicates direction of flow)
- Buildings — Bruin
- Public buildings (selected)
- Bus or coach station
- Coniferous wood
- Non-coniferous wood
- Mixed wood
- Orchard
- Park or ornamental grounds
- Chimney or tower
- Glasshouse
- Graticule intersection at 5' intervals
- Heliport (H)
- Triangulation pillar
- Windmill with or without sails
- Spoil heap, refuse tip or dump
- Windpump
- Radio or TV mast
- Church or Chapel { with tower / with spire / without tower or spire }
- Quarry

BOUNDARIES

- National
- County, Region or Islands Area
- London Borough
- District
- NT National Trust
- FC Forestry Commission
- NT always open
- NT opening restricted
- Pedestrians only - observe local signs
- NTS (in red or blue) National Trust for Scotland
- National Park or Forest Park

HEIGHTS AND ROCK FEATURES

outcrop, cliff, scree

Contours are at 10 metres vertical interval
•144 Heights are to the nearest metre above mean sea level
Heights shown close to a triangulation pillar refer to the station height at ground level and not necessarily to the summit.

RAILWAYS

- Track multiple or single
- Track narrow gauge
- Bridges, Footbridge
- Tunnel
- Viaduct
- Freight line, siding or tramway
- Station (a) principal (b) closed to passengers
- Level crossing — LC
- Embankment
- Cutting

TOURIST INFORMATION

- Information centre
- Parking
- Picnic site
- Selected places of tourist interest
- Telephone, public/motoring organisation
- Golf course or links
- Public convenience (in rural areas) — PC
- Viewpoint
- Camp site
- Caravan site
- Youth hostel

ANTIQUITIES

- VILLA Roman
- Castle Non-Roman
- Battlefield (with date)
- + Position of antiquity which cannot be drawn to scale
- ☆ Tumulus
- M Ancient Monuments and Historic Buildings in the care of the Secretaries of State for the Environment, for Scotland and for Wales and that are open to the public

The revision date of archaeological information varies over the sheet

ABBREVIATIONS

P	Post office	CH	Clubhouse
PH	Public house	PC	Public convenience (in rural areas)
MS	Milestone MP Milepost	TH	Town Hall, Guildhall or equivalent
		CG	Coastguard

SCALE 1:50 000
Kilometres 2 1 0 1 2 3
Miles 1 0 1 2

VARIATIONS FOUND ON FIRST SERIES MAPS

- Multiple } Standard gauge track
- Single
- Narrow gauge
- Level crossing
- Low water mark
- High water mark
- .T .A .R Telephone call box
- PO
- AA
- RAC
- Civil Parish or equivalent
- National
- Dual carriageway
- Road under construction
- Road used as a public path
- Footpath
- Windmill (in use)
- Windmill (disused)
- Glasshouse
- Park or ornamental grounds
- Bracken, heath and rough grassland
- Dunes
- Open pit
- Electricity transmission line (with pylons spaced conventionally)
- Broadcasting station (mast or tower)

Key Sheet 1:50 000

Map Extract 6

Gateshead   Sheet 88   1:50 000 Second Series

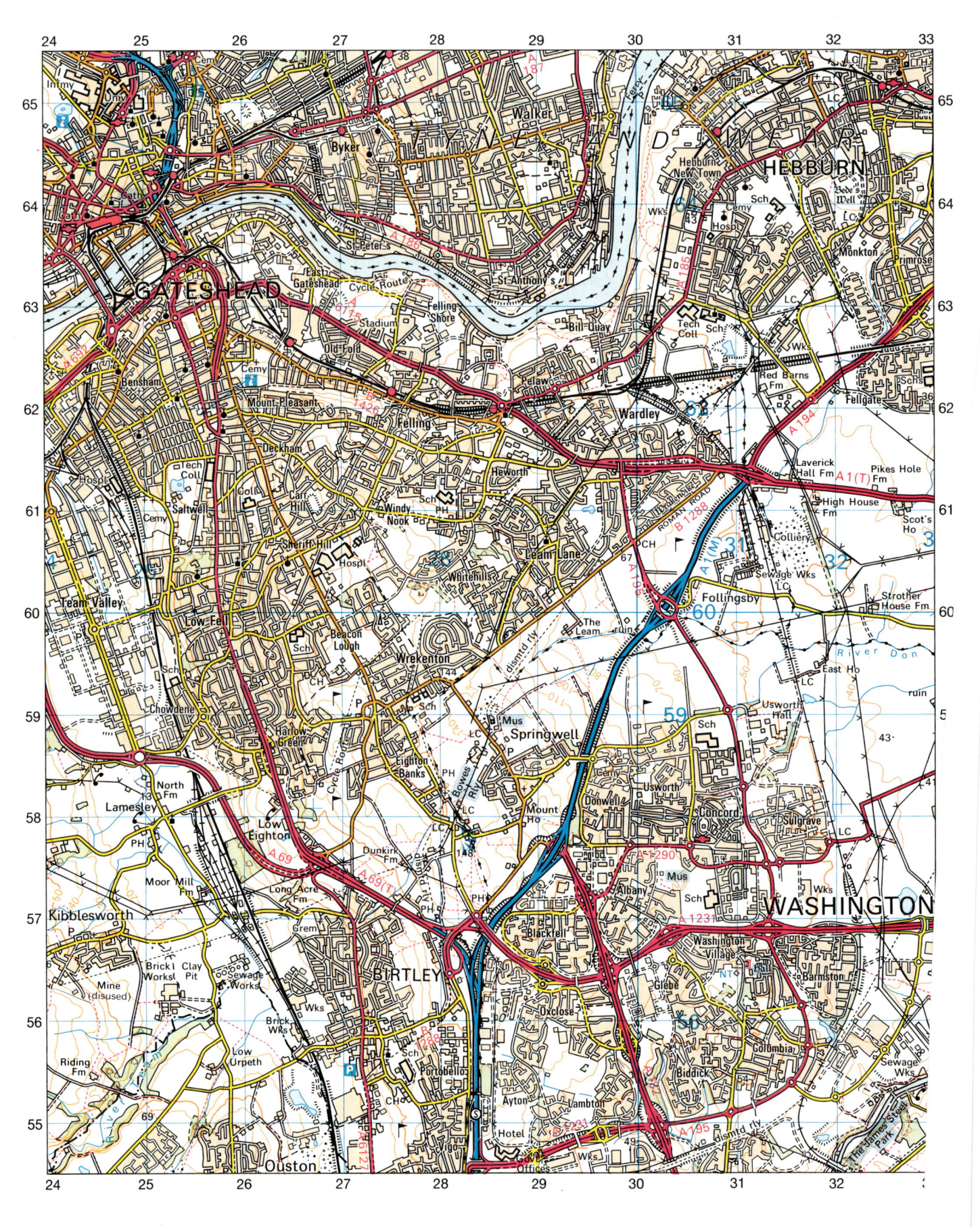

Map Extract 11

Sevenoaks, Kent Sheet 188 1:50 000 Second Series

Map Extract 12

ROADS

===== Road   ----- Track   - - - - Path

The representation on this map of a road, track or path is no evidence of the existence of a right of way

HEIGHTS

Values are given in metres above mean sea level at Newlyn.

Surface heights determined by { ground survey .163m
air survey .108m

Bench mark and value   BM 151·36m

Bench mark lists containing fuller and possibly later levelling information are obtainable from the Ordnance Survey.

Contours may be shown at 5 metre, 10 metre, 25 feet or a varying vertical interval.

RAILWAYS

Cutting, Embankment, Multiple track, Road over, Single track, Road under, Level crossing, Foot Bridge, Siding tramway or mineral line — Standard gauge

Narrow gauge

ROCK FEATURES

Loose rock, Boulders, Outcrop, Scree, Vertical face
150m 160m 200m

GENERAL FEATURES

- Antiquity, (site of)
- Boulders (isolated or coastal)
- Building: important building
- Glasshouse
- Electricity transmission line
- Triangulation station
- Direction of flow of water
- Chalk pit, clay pit or quarry
- Gravel pit
- Sand pit
- Refuse or slag heap
- Sand
- Shingle
- Sloping masonry
- Lake, loch or pond

VEGETATION

- Scrub
- Heath
- Marsh
- Saltings
- Reeds
- Bracken, rough grassland
- Coppice
- Orchard
- Coniferous trees
- Non-coniferous trees

In some areas bracken and rough grassland are shown separately

ABBREVIATIONS

BH	Beer House	Pol Sta	Police Station
BP	Boundary Post	PO	Post Office
BS	Boundary Stone	PC	Public Convenience
Ch	Church	PH	Public House
CH	Club House	PW	Place of Worship
F Sta	Fire Station	S	Stone
FB	Foot Bridge	Spr	Spring
Fn	Fountain	TCB	Telephone Call Box
GP	Guide Post	TCP	Telephone Call Post
MP, MS	Mile Post, Mile Stone	TH	Town Hall
NTL	Normal Tidal Limit	W	Well
P	Pole or Post	Y	Youth hostel

BOUNDARIES

- County (England and Wales)   Region or Islands Area (Scotland)
- District
- London Borough
- Civil Parish (England), Community (Wales)
- Constituency (County, Borough, Burgh or European Assembly) Electoral Division or Ward (shown only on sheets containing areas not published at larger scales)
- 0·91m FF   CF   Example of change of mereing (shown only where there is no publication at larger scales)

Imperial equivalents for metric boundary mereings: 0·91m = 3ft   1·22m = 4ft

Coincident boundaries are shown by the first appropriate symbol above, e.g. Boro Const & ED Bdy For Ordnance Survey purposes County Boundary is deemed to be the limit of the parish structure whether or not a parish area adjoins

SCALE 1:10 000

Metres 100 0 100 500 1000 1500 Metres
500 0 500 1000 2000 3000 4000 5000 Feet

Key Sheet 1:10 000

Map Extract 15

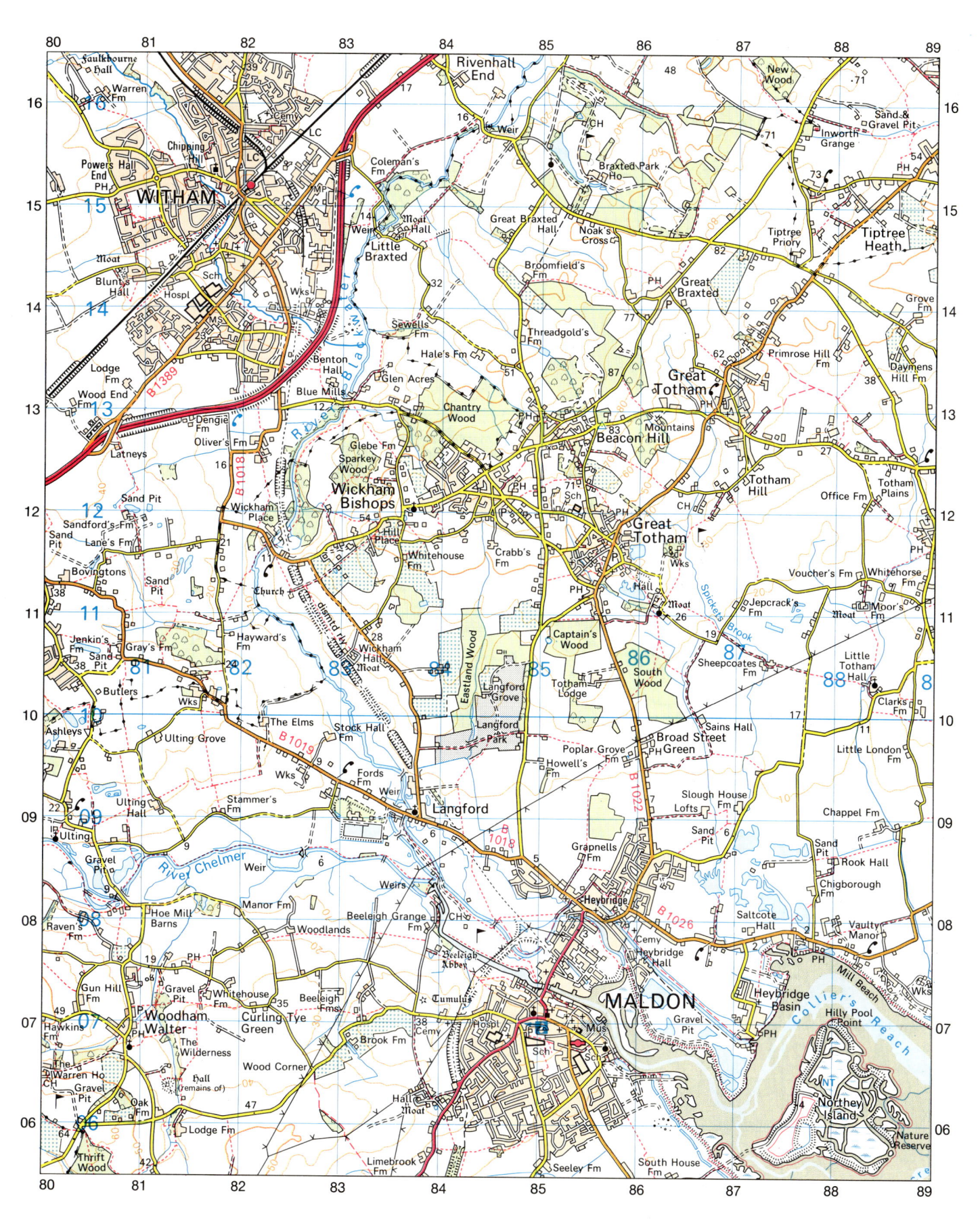

Maldon, Essex   Sheet 168   1:50 000 Second Series

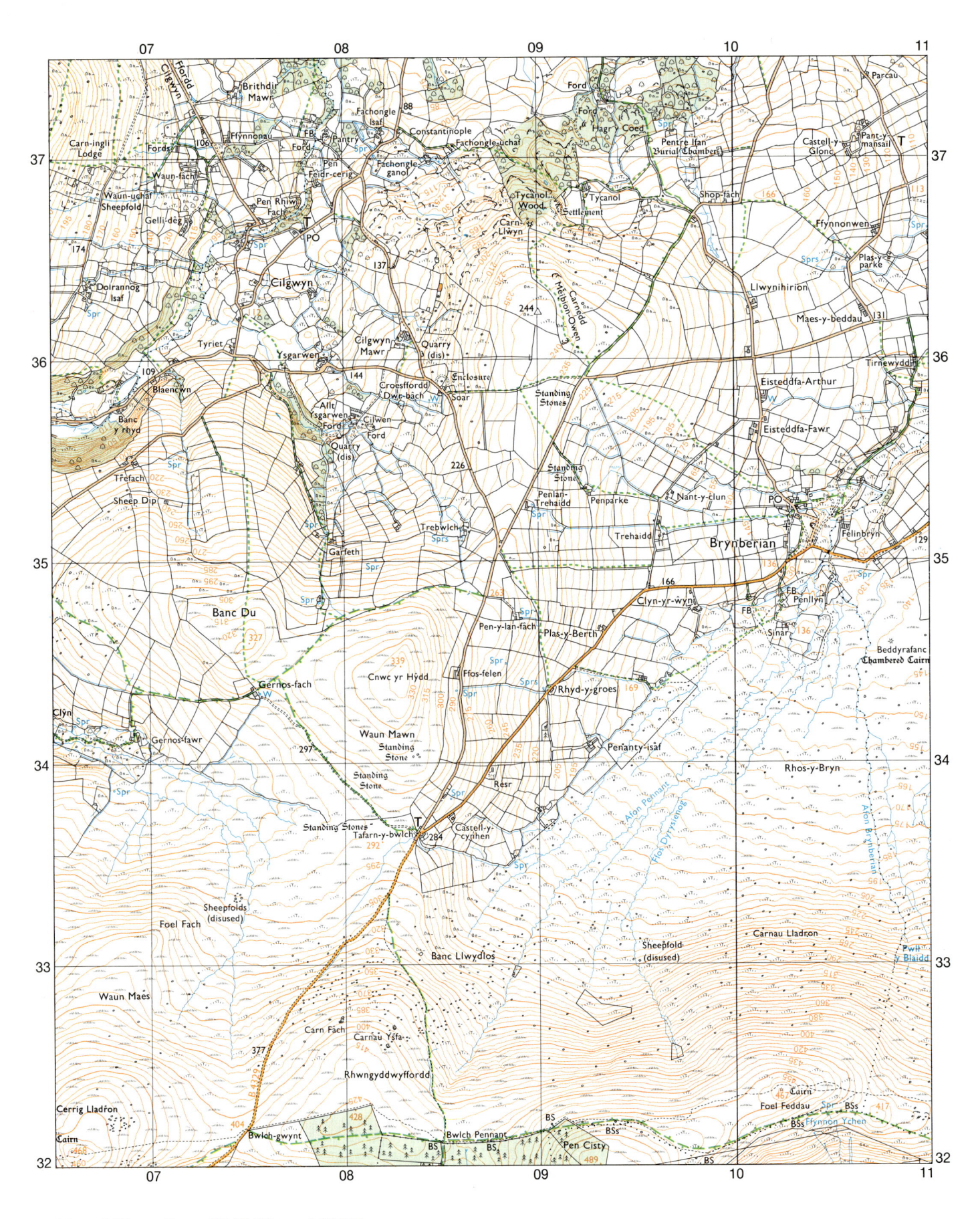

Map Extract 16

Mynydd Preseli   SN 03/13   1:25 000

Route race

(Use any map.)

Choose two places on the map. With your partner see who can find:
(i) the shortest route by car or by bike;
(ii) the shortest route on foot;
(iii) the route with the least steep gradients between the two places;
(iv) What was the total height climbed?

Pollution

(Use Map Extract 13.)

Leaking drums of highly poisonous liquid have been left behind one of the isolated buildings south of grid line 06.

Play a 'battleships' type game with a partner:
(i) Both decide separately where the drums are hidden. Make a note of the four-figure reference of the square, and the six-figure reference of the building.
(ii) Take turns to search – first use four-figure references to find the square – landing in a square next to it is a near miss and you must tell your partner. When you locate the square use six-figure references to find the exact building.

First to find the other's drums is the winner.

Emergency

(i) (Use Map Extract 7.) You are out trekking on a winter's day when your friend slips on the way up Low Buzzard Knot (0925) and breaks an ankle and cannot be moved. You have to get back to telephone for help. Above 400 m the snow is deep. The day started clear and sunny but now thick clouds are appearing. It is 2 p.m. already.

Describe the route of your journey back, the hazards you meet, and what happens.

Which of the rules in Fig. 78 would have helped you most?

(ii) (Use Map Extract 13.) Your friend's car breaks down on the unfenced road by Sunbiggin Tarn during heavy rain and gale-force winds. What will you do?

Where is it?

(Use Map Extract 16 and Fig. 77.)

The descriptions in Fig. 77 all refer to this map extract:
(i) What is the name of the house where the holiday cottage is?
(ii) Where is the picnic spot and what is it?

(i) The holiday cottage is situated in a valley on the northern slopes of the Preseli Hills, only 10 minutes from the sea. It is attached to a farmstead and sleeps six. Water is fetched from a stream that flows past the back of the house. Across the stream only one field separates you from the freedom of the open mountain. The cottage is approached by half a kilometre of walled narrow road, and lies 185 m above sea level.

(ii) You cannot reach the picnic area without walking. You get a beautiful view of the valley down to Brynberian. The rough way is straight out of the cottage and across the stream, through the field and over the wall, across three more streams, then climb straight up 65 metres height. You can't miss it.

Fig. 77 Descriptions for 'Where is it?'

---

1 Wear warm waterproof clothing and boots.
2 Always carry a compass, map and whistle.
3 Carry emergency kit – rations, survival bag and arctic tent, ice axe and rope.
4 Always go with several companions.
5 Ask about the weather forecast.
6 Leave details of your proposed route with friends or someone who will notice if you do not return on time.

Fig. 78 Mountain walking in winter.

Rural land use

Fig. 79 Langdale, looking east from 268058, Map Extract 7.

Rural land use includes farming, forestry and 'natural' vegetation. Orchards, rough pasture, greenhouses, field boundaries, etc. may be marked on maps as information about land use.

1. Study each of the Key Sheets (Map Extracts 5 and 8). Make a table with five columns – one each for: 1:50 000 First Series; 1:50 000 Second Series; 1:63 360 Tourist; 1:25 000; 1:25 000 Leisure.
   In each column list all the things that show rural land use on that map.

2. Which map or maps give the most information about rural land use?

   Several different land uses are visible in the photograph (Fig. 79) looking down Langdale. The lightest colour fields have been cut for silage (green animal fodder), the darkest fields are grazed pasture, and the mid-coloured fields are waiting to be cut.
   The river confluence is at GR 279059 on Map Extract 7. Stool End is visible in the bottom right-hand corner.

3. Trace the field boundaries in the area east of easting 275, and between northings 053 and 063. Mark on the land use in the fields that you can see on the photograph.

4. Use the map and photograph to describe the land-use above the valley floor. Why are there so few field boundaries on the sides of the valley?

   It is possible to use the information on OS maps to classify land by its use. Fig. 80 suggests a classification for use with OS 1:50 000 maps. The problem is with category 7, which is blank on the map, and may be rough pasture, pasture, or arable land. You have to use clues, especially the relief of the land, to guess which is most likely.

5. Use Map Extract 15. (i) Draw a frame on tracing paper for the eight squares bounded by grid lines eastings 84 and 88, and northings 10 and 12. (ii) Mark on the land use categories 1 to 6 only (Fig. 80). (iii) The rest of the area is category 7! Fig. 81 gives you some idea of the agriculture there.

1 Urban and industrial	5 Glasshouses
2 Forest and woodland	6 Marshland
3 Orchards	7 Other open land
4 Parkland	

Fig. 80 Land use categories for 1:50 000 OS maps.

Fig. 81 Looking east from 862114 on Map Extract 15. The bird-scarer is in a strawberry field. Wheat fields are in the background.

A land use transect

Transects are based on cross-sections. Fig. 82 is a land use transect across Langdale Valley down easting 28 between northings 05 and 07. Most of it is visible on Fig. 79 as well. The diagram helps to show the relationships between land use, relief etc. listed for each heading.

Transects are most useful as records of fieldwork. Other headings can be used (e.g. soil types, industrial activity) and a transect need not be a straight line – it can follow a road or footpath.

6 Describe the relationships between land use, field size, relief features and altitude along the transect in Fig. 82.

Fig. 82 Land use transect, Map Extract 7.

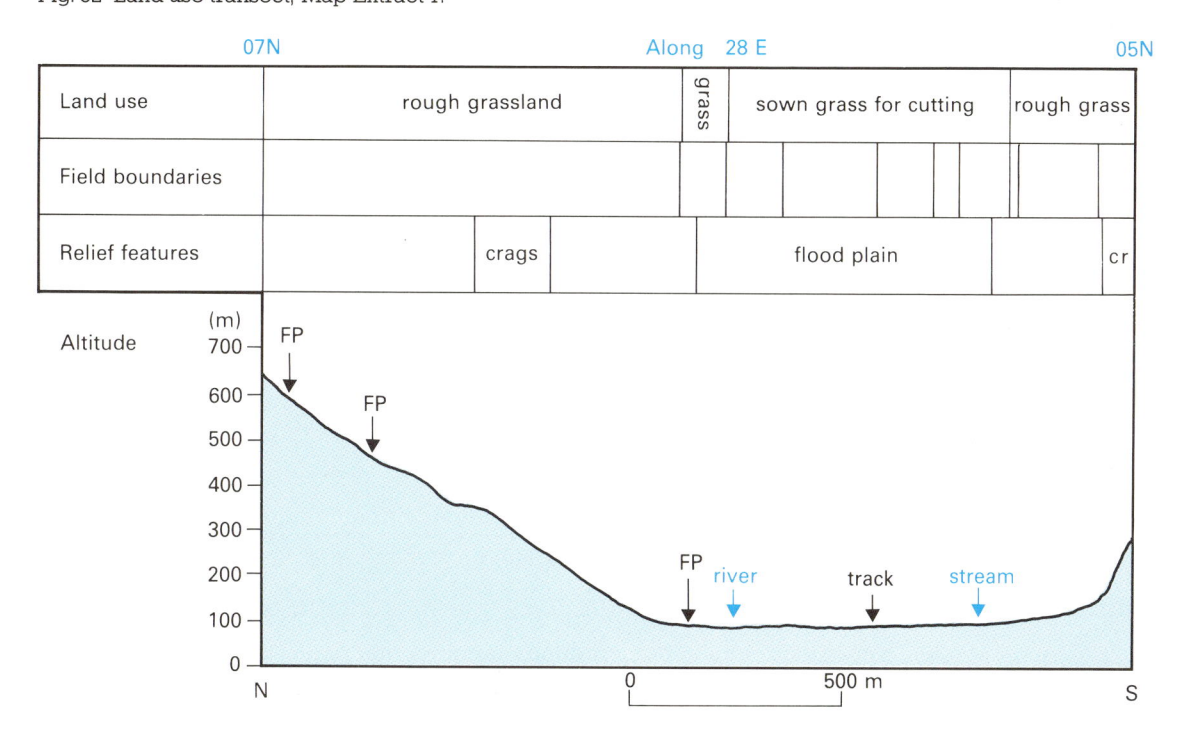

Distribution of settlements

Small settlements usually serve the area just around them, but large settlements have often grown up to serve large areas that include several smaller settlements. So the most obvious feature of the distribution of settlements is that large settlements are further apart from each other than are small ones.

1 Fig. 83 shows the distribution of settlements on Map Extract 11. (i) What problems are there in deciding which areas to shade in as built-up? (ii) What are the differences between villages and hamlets?

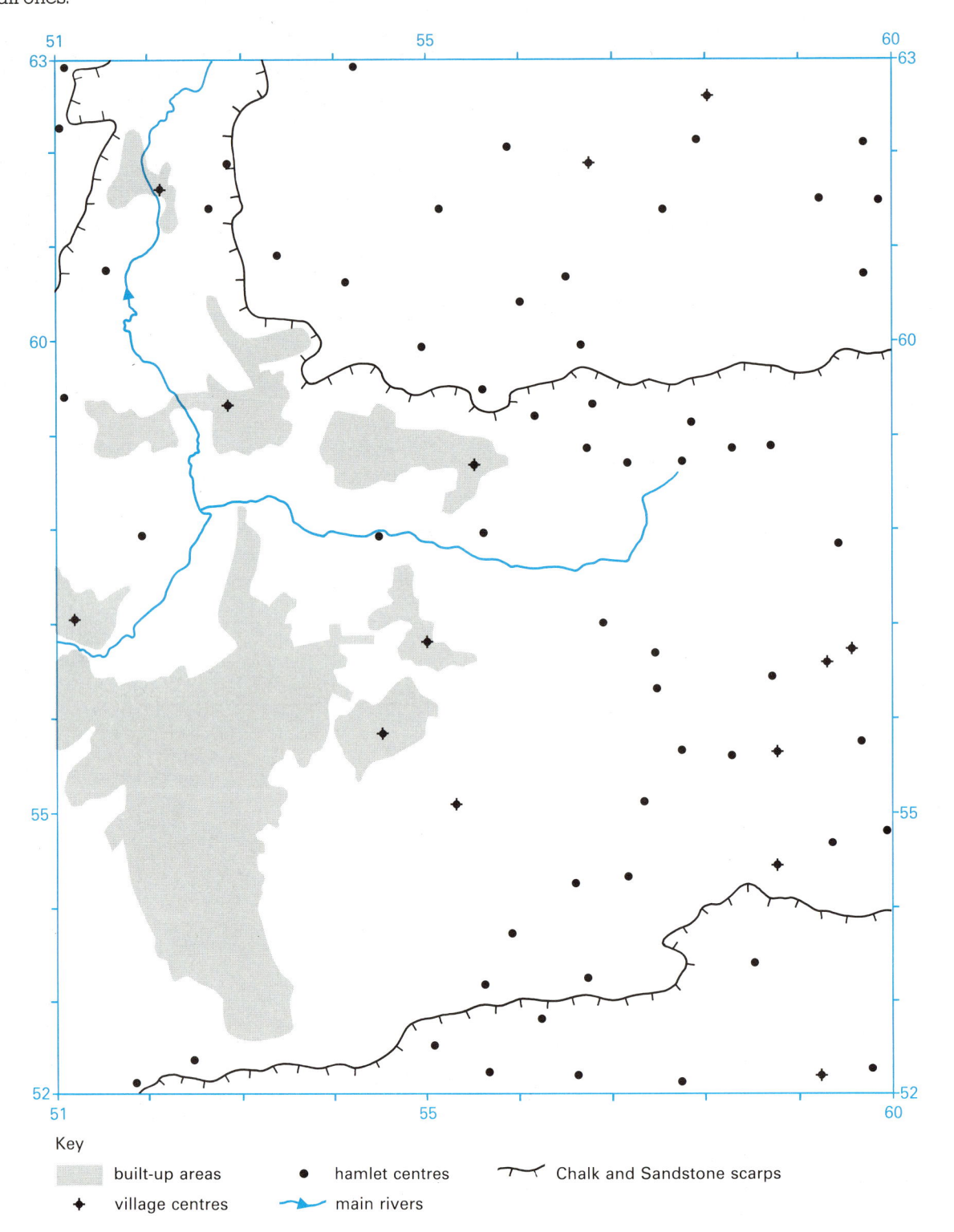

Key
- built-up areas
- village centres
- hamlet centres
- main rivers
- Chalk and Sandstone scarps

Fig. 83 Settlements on Map Extract 11.

2 Look at Map Extract 15. Decide which settlements you would classify as towns (see page 30). Measure the distance from each to the nearest other town. What is the average distance between towns?
3 Put a piece of tracing paper over Map Extract 15 and mark in the coastline. (i) Shade in the built-up areas. (ii) Mark the centres of all villages and hamlets as on Fig. 83. (iii) Estimate the distance between them and their nearest neighbour. (iv) How do the distances compare with those between towns?
4 Study your tracing. (i) Join up any settlements that seem to be located in a line. (ii) Draw a circle round any area in which there are a lot of settlements close together. (iii) Draw another line around areas where there are very few settlements.
5 Look at the map extract and see if there is some evidence to explain these patterns.
6 Use Map Extract 13, an area with fewer people per square kilometre, and do Exercises 3, 4 and 5 again. This time include **all** settlements on your tracing, i.e. even isolated buildings that you think are homes.
7 Draw a sketch map of Map Extract 13 and mark in the main roads. (i) Shade in the areas where a lot of people live. (ii) Use another shading for areas where few people live. (iii) Leave empty areas blank.
8 Annotate your sketch map with reasons to explain this **distribution of population**.

Growth of settlements

You can see how much settlements have grown by looking at maps drawn in the past.

Fig. 84 is from a 1″ to the mile OS map first published in 1819 (revised in 1864). It shows the area west of easting 28 on Map Extract 6, and has been enlarged to 1:50 000 so that it is easy to compare.

1 Estimate the increase in urban area on Fig. 84 over the 120 years – is it 25%, 50%, 100%, 200%?
2 Count the urbanised (built-up) square kilometres on each map. How near was your first estimate?
3 Draw a sketch map of Fig. 84. Mark on the River Tyne. (i) Shade in the area built up in 1864. (ii) Use a different shading to show the area that is now built-up on Map Extract 6. (iii) Mark on arrows to show the main directions in which areas have grown since 1864. (iv) How much of this growth is related to transport routes?
4 In a different colour mark in the areas you think will be built-up by 2085. Explain your forecast.
5 Look at Map Extract 11. Draw a traced sketch map showing the area you think was built-up in 1865. You can compare your ideas with reality by looking at the First Edition (1864) of OS 1″ Sheet 80 Sevenoaks, republished by David and Charles in 1970.

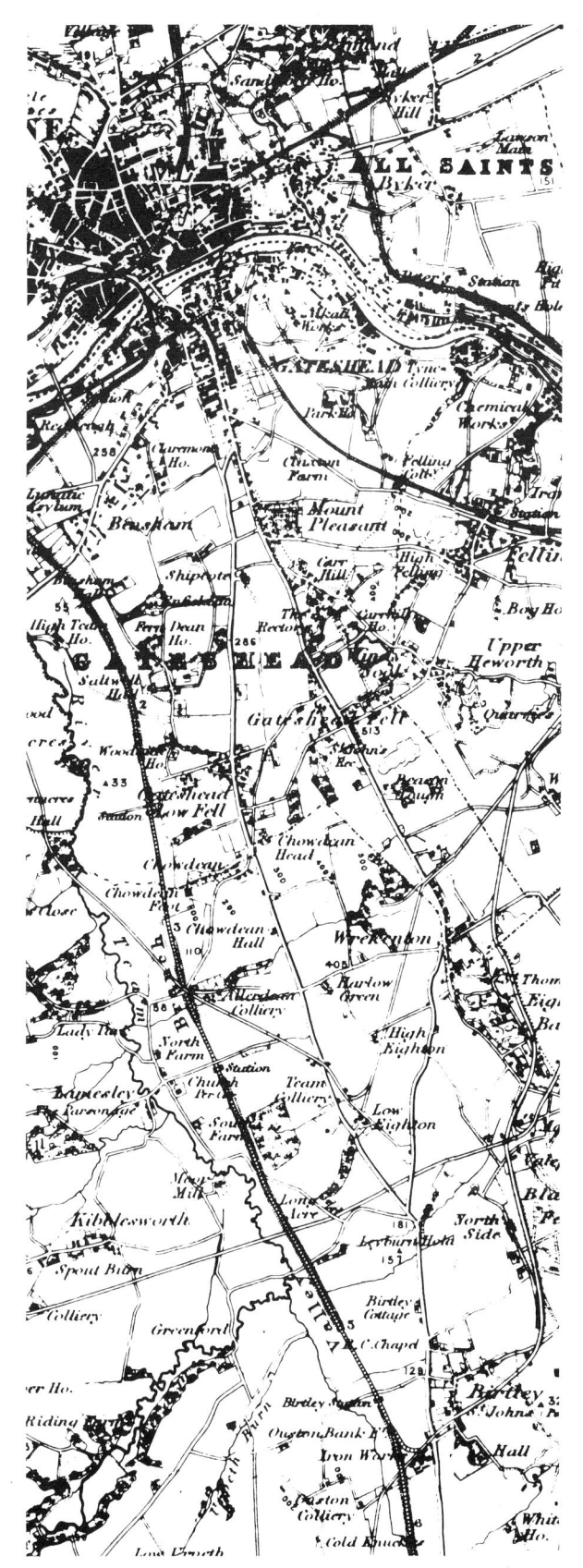

Fig. 84 Part of OS 1″ First Edition 1819 (revised in 1864), No. 6, enlarged to scale 1:50 000.

Communications and transport

Most lines of communication and transport are marked on OS maps.

1. Study the key to OS 1:50 000 Second Series maps (Map Extract 5). List all the lines of communication or transport shown. What travels along each line? What important lines of communication are not shown? (Clue: listen and see.) What lines of transport are not shown? (Clue: drink and smell.)

Road transport

2. Draw a sketch map of Map Extract 15 to show the pattern of A and B roads in the area. Annotate it to show which settlements the network serves.
3. Which settlements are particularly well served by the main road network? Why is this?
4. On Map Extract 11 how would the motorway shown affect people living in (i) Kemsing (5558) and (ii) West Kingsdown (5762)?
5. From Map Extract 1 draw an annotated sketch map showing all the roads and footpaths within 2 km of Prior's Norton (8624) that are used by people travelling to and from the village. Suggest reasons for people using each route.
6. You live at Brawn Farm (8224) and your friend lives at Norton Court Farm (8624). Give him or her instructions to get to your home (i) on foot (ii) by bicycle (iii) in a 20-tonne lorry with trailer.
7. With a partner choose a map extract. Select a 'home' for yourself. Your partner tells you where he or she lives. Give your partner directions to visit you, as though they had no map. Can your partner find out where you live?

Fig. 85 is a sketch map showing how many people travel to work in Gloucester from each of the surrounding areas.

8. Look at Map Extract 1. (i) Which roads will be busiest each morning and evening? (People using the M5 from the north of Gloucester would leave it near Cheltenham to come in on the A40(T).) (ii) From which areas are people likely to use the train? (iii) At which road junctions would you expect traffic jams?

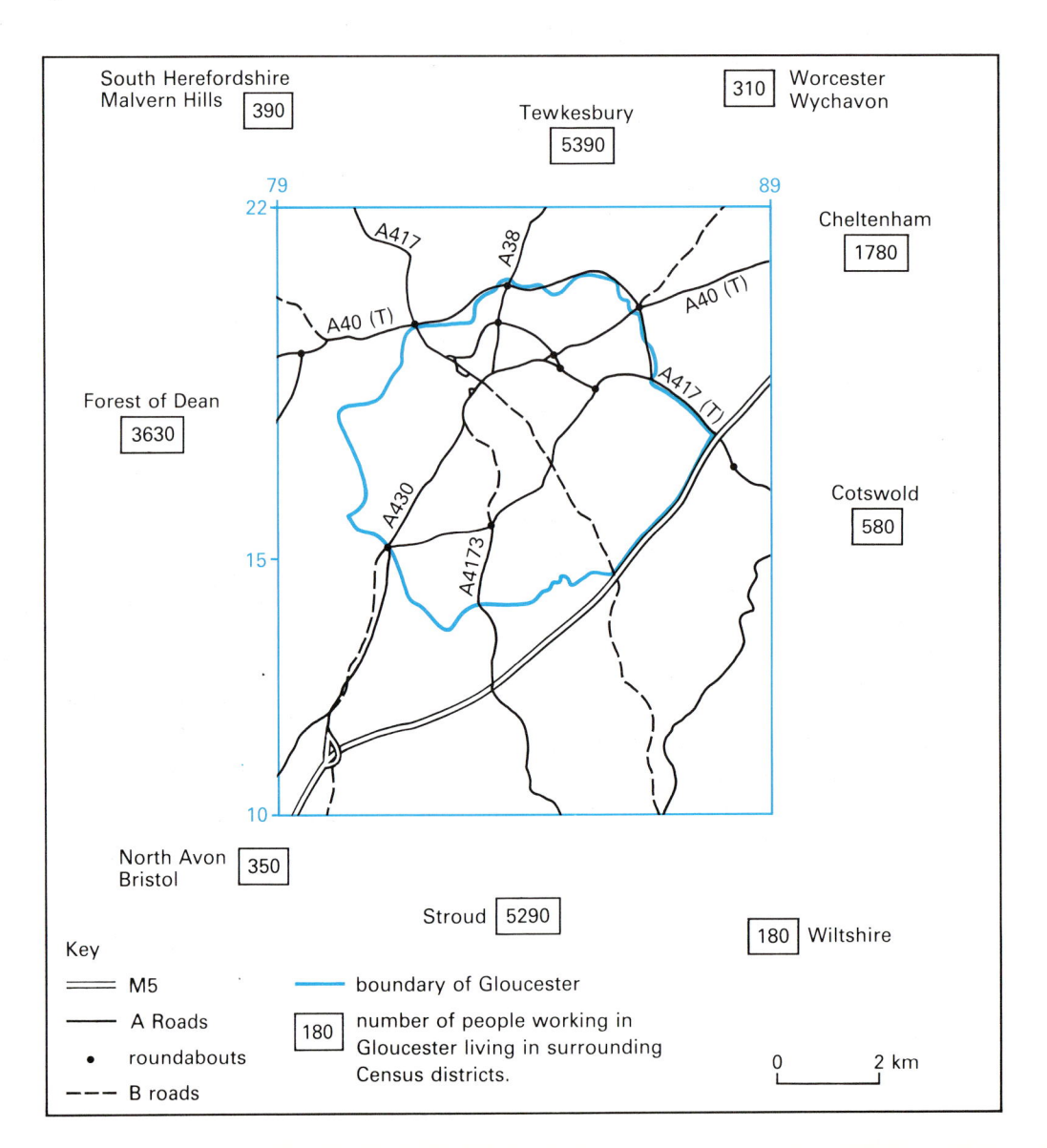

Fig. 85 People commuting to Gloucester.

Now look at Map Extract 15. Mrs Milton lives at Great Totham Hall (8611) and works at the hospital in Maldon. Fig. 86 describes her journey.

9 Follow Mrs Milton's journey on the map and suggest explanations for (i) to (viii) in Fig. 86.

> I get the car out at 7.30 a.m. Last night's deep snowfall has not been cleared off the road to the village (i), and I nearly go off the road into a field. There is less snow in the village and more tyre tracks to follow (ii), and once I turn left onto the B1022 things are much better (iii). But not for long – by the pub at Broad Street Green I arrive at the end of a tail-back (iv). It takes 20 minutes to reach the junction with the B1026. Things are no better now (v). Once across the bridge at least the traffic is moving, but very slowly (vi). Over the next bridge, another wait (vii), then turn right and at last I'm shifting – for the last 400 metres (viii)! Late again.

Fig. 86 Mrs Milton's journey to work.

Railways

Railways are an important part of many landscapes and clearly shown on OS maps. The area south of Newcastle on Map Extract 6 is one such landscape.

10 Make a free-hand map or tracing of the railways on Map Extract 6, using the same symbols as the map.
11 On your map mark the factories, mines, etc. that are located near a railway line and are able to use it (they need a station, siding or special line).
12 Number each example and explain how each is connected to the main rail network and what they probably use it for.

Waterways and ports

Few rivers and streams, or even canals, are navigable by large boats, though most can be travelled by canoe or rowing boat. Fig. 87 shows some of the waterways on Map Extract 2. Gloucester docks are no longer very important for commerical traffic, but are used by leisure craft.

13 Make a copy of Fig. 87. Mark on all obstacles to navigation shown on Map Extract 2. Label the canal, docks and bridges. Shade in tidal water.
14 Where would you expect to find a lock?
15 Would river traffic use the West or the East Channel of the River Severn to go north from Gloucester? Explain your answer.
16 Complete your map by showing how other forms of transport link to the water transport in the area.
17 Use your library to find out about the Severn Bore and the Sharpness Canal.

Transport and industrial location

Sites for industry are often closely related to transport facilities. The table (Fig. 88) describes three factories and three locations.

18 Which factory would you site at each location?
19 Draw a sketch map of your idea for each site, annotating them to explain your decisions.

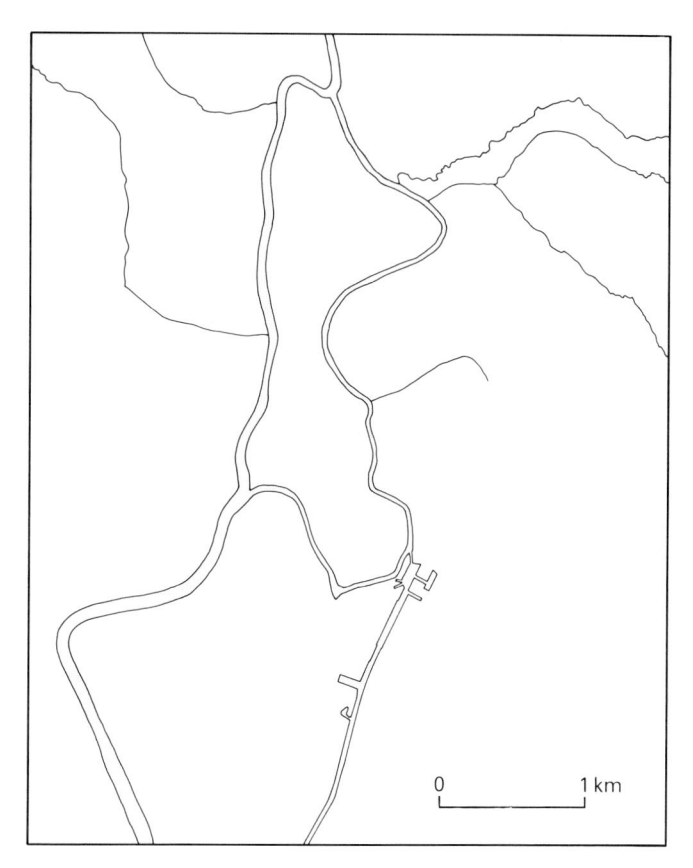

Fig. 87 Waterways on Map Extract 2.

Factories
1 A sawmill where tree trunks will be sawn into timber for the building trade.
2 A coal-fired power station producing electricity for the National Grid.
3 A factory where foods will be packaged for distribution to shops and supermarkets.
A A 'green field' site next to a motorway junction, about 10 km from a town.
B The site of a demolished warehouse alongside a canal dock. Barges still use the canal and the site is near to main roads on the edge of a town.
C A site on the banks of a large river in the countryside. A main line railway passes nearby.

Fig. 88 Locations for factories.

DIAGRAMS, MAPS AND DATA

So far this book has mainly studied Ordnance Survey maps and air photographs. It has tried to help you to understand the basic skills of map reading, and has gone on to help you to interpret what you read on maps.

There are many other kinds of maps and diagrams and the next section of this book aims to help you to understand some of the maps and diagrams that are more frequently used in school. Many of the examples are taken from examination papers – sorry about that – but they could prove useful!

It may be helpful to identify maps that are often used, but not produced by the Ordnance Survey. Some are very well known – for example the diagrammatic map of the London Underground.

1 List five different maps (not produced by the Ordnance Survey) that you have come across. They may be used by you or your family.

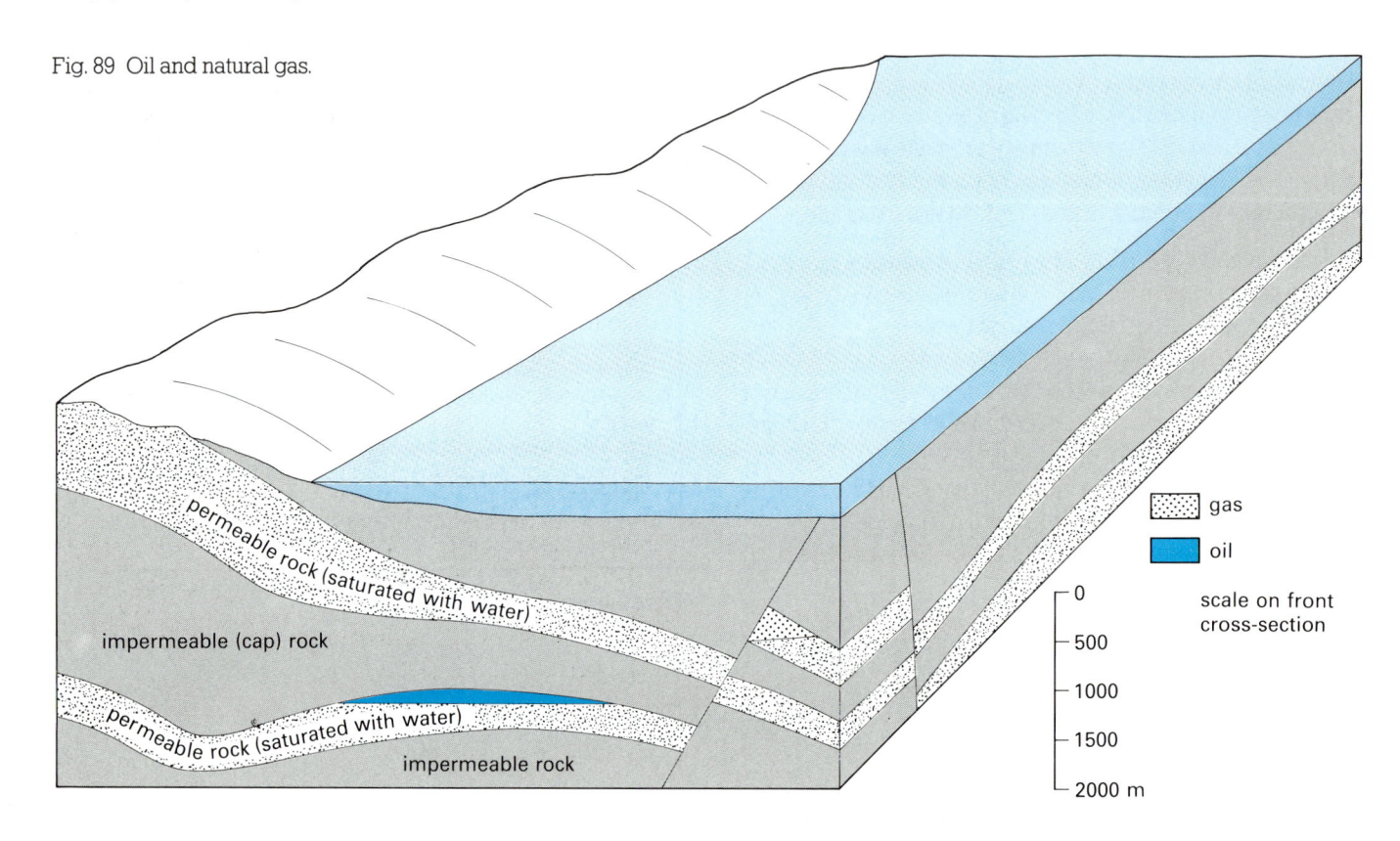

Fig. 89 Oil and natural gas.

Blocks and crosses

In this section **geological cross-sections** and **block diagrams** are used to explore the location of water, oil and gas under the ground.

Oil and gas traps

Geological cross-sections and block diagrams are often used in geography to explain the way in which surface features and economic activities are related to underlying rocks.

Fig. 89 is a fairly typical geological block diagram. Notice the way in which the front of the block diagram is actually a slice through the earth's crust – a cross-section – like the cross-sections in Figs. 90 and 91.

This block diagram is intended to show the way in which oil and natural gas can be trapped underground between layers (or strata) of permeable rock and impermeable rock. Both oil and gas tend to be trapped above a layer of water, sometimes together as in Figs. 90 and 91, sometimes separately as in Fig. 89.

Remember that the traps are not hollow. They are solid rock but all the tiny pore spaces are filled with petroleum gas or oil instead of air or water.

1. Look at Fig. 89. In what kind of trap is (i) the oil and (ii) the gas?
2. Look at Fig. 89. Where would you site drilling rigs for the extraction of oil? Suggest positions for four rigs.
3. How deep would the sea be at each site?
4. How deep would you expect to drill to reach oil?
5. Where would you site a gas drilling rig?
6. How deep would you have to drill for the gas?
7. How would you get the oil and gas ashore?

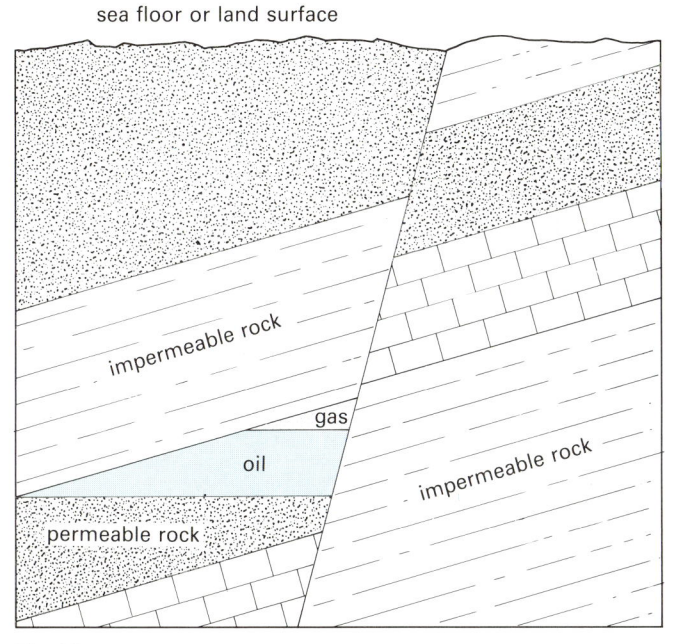

Fig. 90 A fault trap.

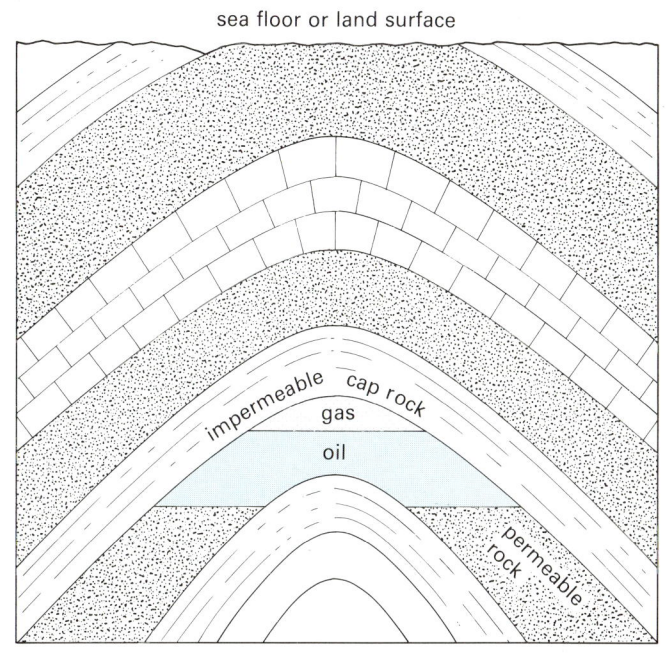

Fig. 91 An anticline trap.

Water and rock structure

Another very common block diagram using geology shows a typical escarpment as in Fig. 92.

8 What is an escarpment?
9 How many escarpments can you identify on Fig. 92?
10 Identify a scarp slope and a dip slope.

Certain types of rock frequently produce escarpments. Although they can occur in association with igneous or metamorphic rocks, they are most commonly found on sedimentary rocks that are resistant to erosion in some way. Typically they occur in rocks that have either flat or gently tilted beds or strata (look back at page 34).

11 Study the block diagram in Fig. 92 and explain why the main river flows over an area of clay.
12 The main tributary is fed by four smaller streams. Give the name for the line at which all their sources are located, and explain why this occurs.

A block diagram can help to explain the location of people's activities. You have already seen this in relation to oil rigs, but it is also true of many other geographical features, including settlement and farming.

13 Draw a sketch map of the surface of the block diagram area shown in Fig. 92.

14 On the sketch map   (i) locate a village and three farms   (ii) decide where you would develop a limestone quarry. Give your reasons for each decision.

Two of the map areas that you have studied – Map Extracts 11 and 13 – show areas with well-developed escarpments. Map Extract 13 shows an area with similar, but not identical geology to Fig. 92.

15 Compare your answers to the last exercise with the location of villages and farms in the northern half of Map Extract 13. What are the differences and similarities between the relief features of the map and the diagram?

In areas which consist of **impermeable** rocks, surface water cannot penetrate into the ground. Rainfall therefore tends to run off across the surface and does not infiltrate the rocks.

Permeable rocks often have some run-off, but most rainwater soaks into the ground. This water penetrates the rock until it reaches a level of saturation – where all the pore spaces are filled. This saturation surface is known as the **water table** and it varies in depth according to season, local relief and geological features.

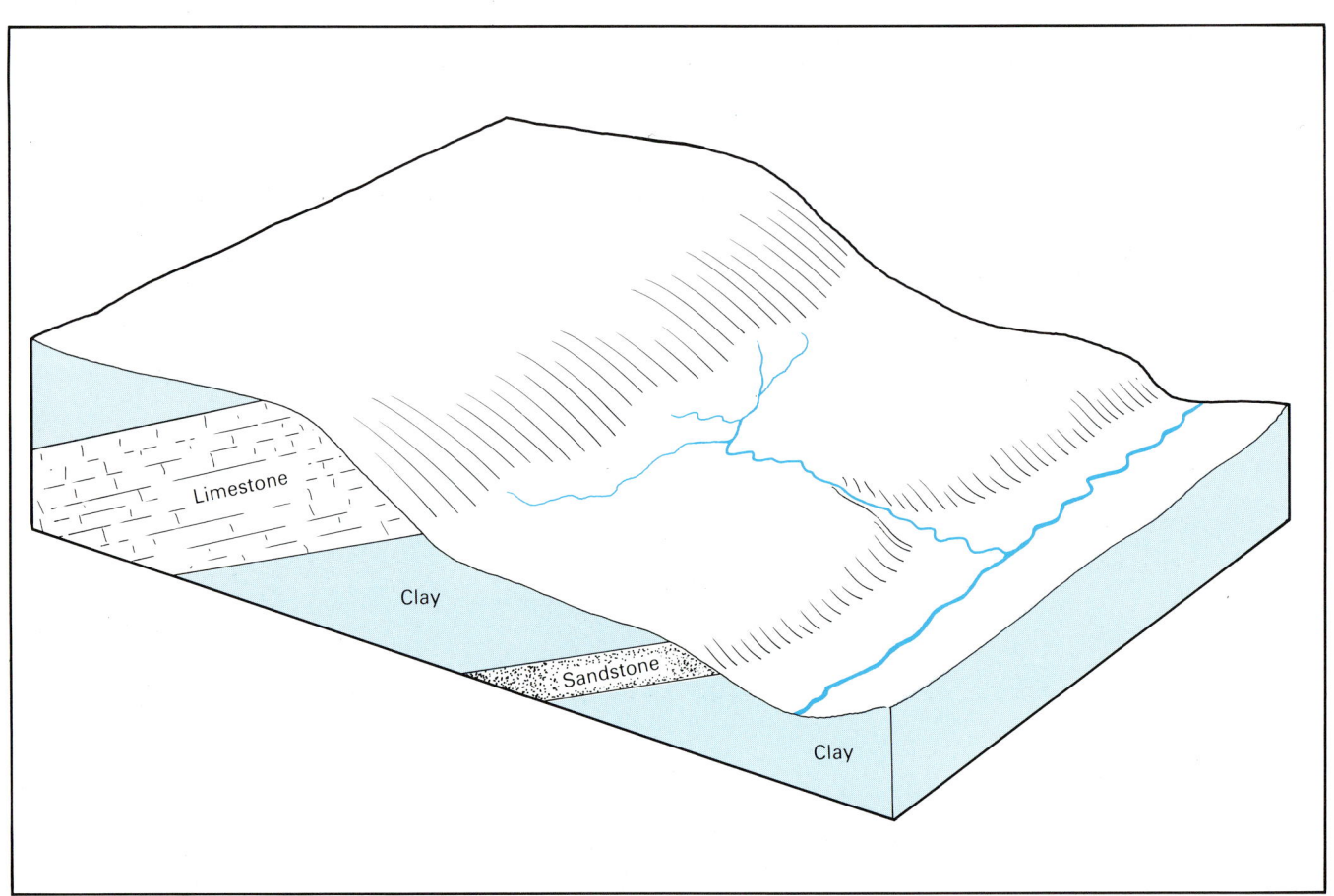

Fig. 92 An escarpment.

16 Using Fig. 93 estimate the height of the source of the tributary flowing down the main slope during (i) summer and (ii) winter. What might be the effect of a severe drought and resultant fall of the water table in the vicinity of the main stream down to the 10 metre level?

On a much wider scale London's water supply is related to the water table. The cross-section of the geology shown in Fig. 94 shows that London is situated in an **artesian basin**. Rainfall over the Chiltern Hills and the North Downs soaks into the permeable chalk rock, and establishes a water table above the level of the site of London. The pressure of this high water table allows water to be extracted easily from wells drilled down through clay to the chalk **aquifer**. One-tenth of London's water is at present obtained in this way.

17 Suggest why over-use of artesian water has made it necessary to use pumps instead of natural pressure to extract water in London. Why are there fears that these wells could run dry?

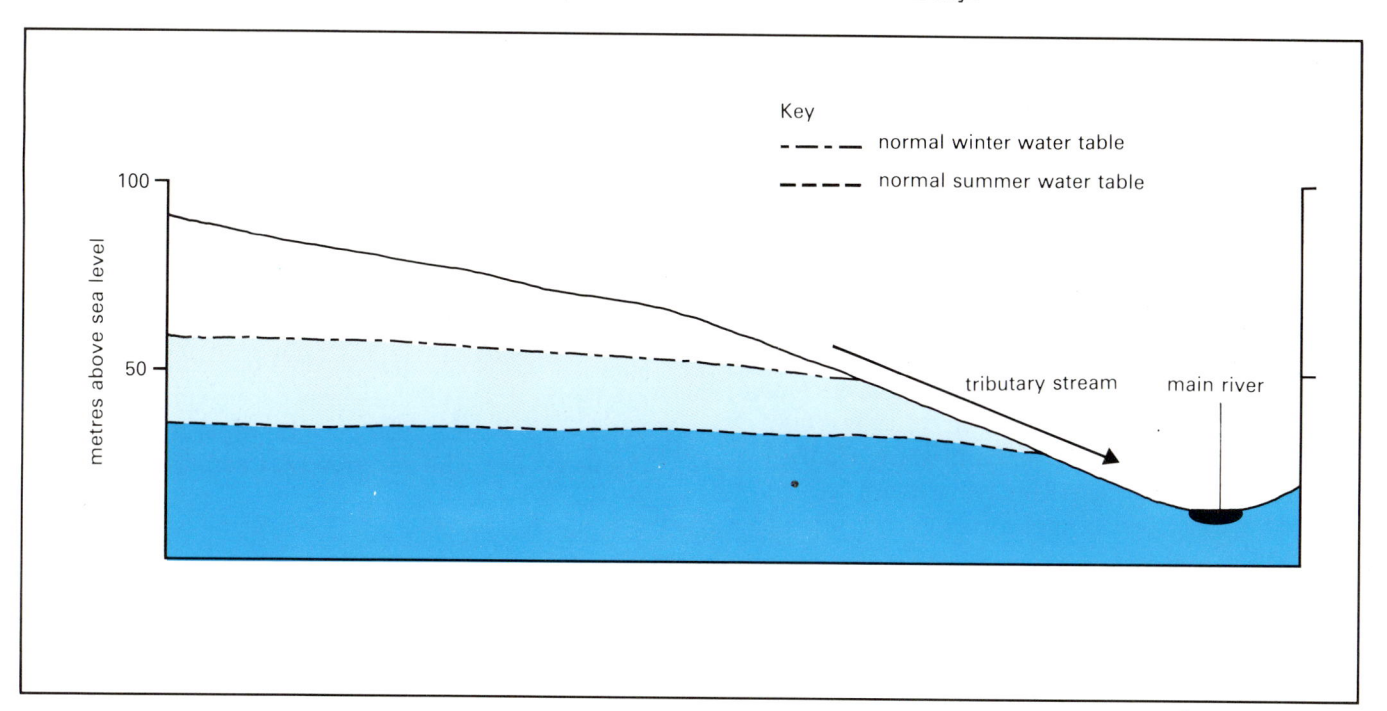

Fig. 93 The water table.

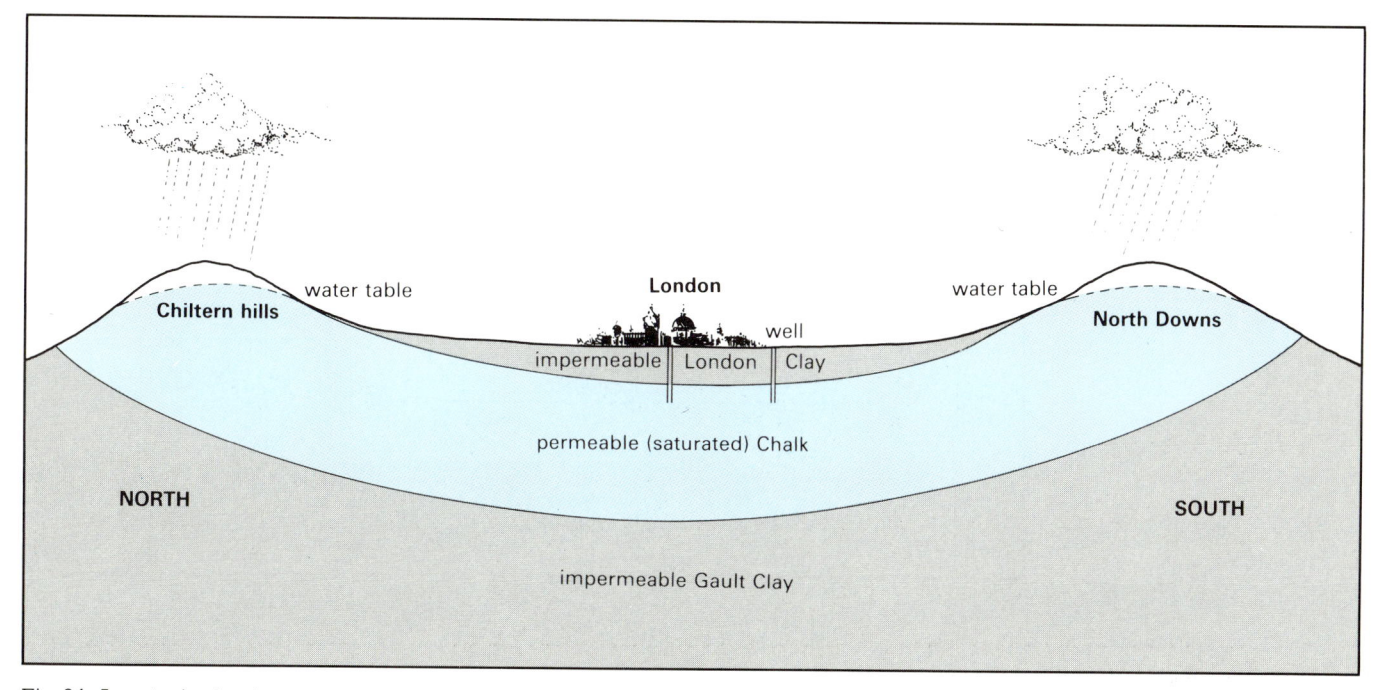

Fig. 94 An artesian basin.

Cycles and flows

Flow diagrams are often used in geography. This section includes some that show circular patterns or cycles.

The water cycle

One of the most common diagrams is the **hydrological cycle** – sometimes called the water cycle. This cycle is illustrated in Fig. 95 and shows how water is exchanged between the earth and the atmosphere.

1 Using Fig. 95 can you identify where in the cycle water is in the following physical states: (i) gas (water vapour), (ii) solid (ice), and (iii) liquid (water)?
2 Can you draw a diagram to show the changes of state between these? Evaporation is an example – the change from liquid to gas.

River basin data

Geographers study many aspects of the hydrological cycle – climate is one example of a major area of interest. On the ground, however, the major unit of study is the river basin. Fig. 96 shows a river basin which is fairly typical of high rainfall coastal areas in western Britain.

3 Place a sheet of tracing paper over Fig. 96. Mark in the streams and add a dotted line to indicate the limit of the river basin – the watershed.
4 Identify and mark on your tracing paper two features that indicate that part of the river basin lies on permeable rock.

The relationship between rainfall and river **discharge** (which is a measure of total **run-off**) is of importance to human activities. Hydrologists are very interested in the measurement of these and other characteristics of river basins. Fig. 97 shows a river catchment graph and records rainfall and discharge for the stream that flows into Slapton Ley on the south Devon coast.

Study the block graph in Fig. 97.

5 In which months does discharge exceed rainfall?
6 Explain why the August discharge is roughly only one-tenth of the month's rainfall. Does this suggest some other measurement which would help to make more sense of the graph?

A little consideration will also help to explain why, in spite of the dramatic monthly differences in rainfall and discharge, it is really the annual balance that matters.

7 Work out the annual difference between rainfall and discharge. Can it be described as a surplus or a deficit?

Fig. 95 The water cycle.

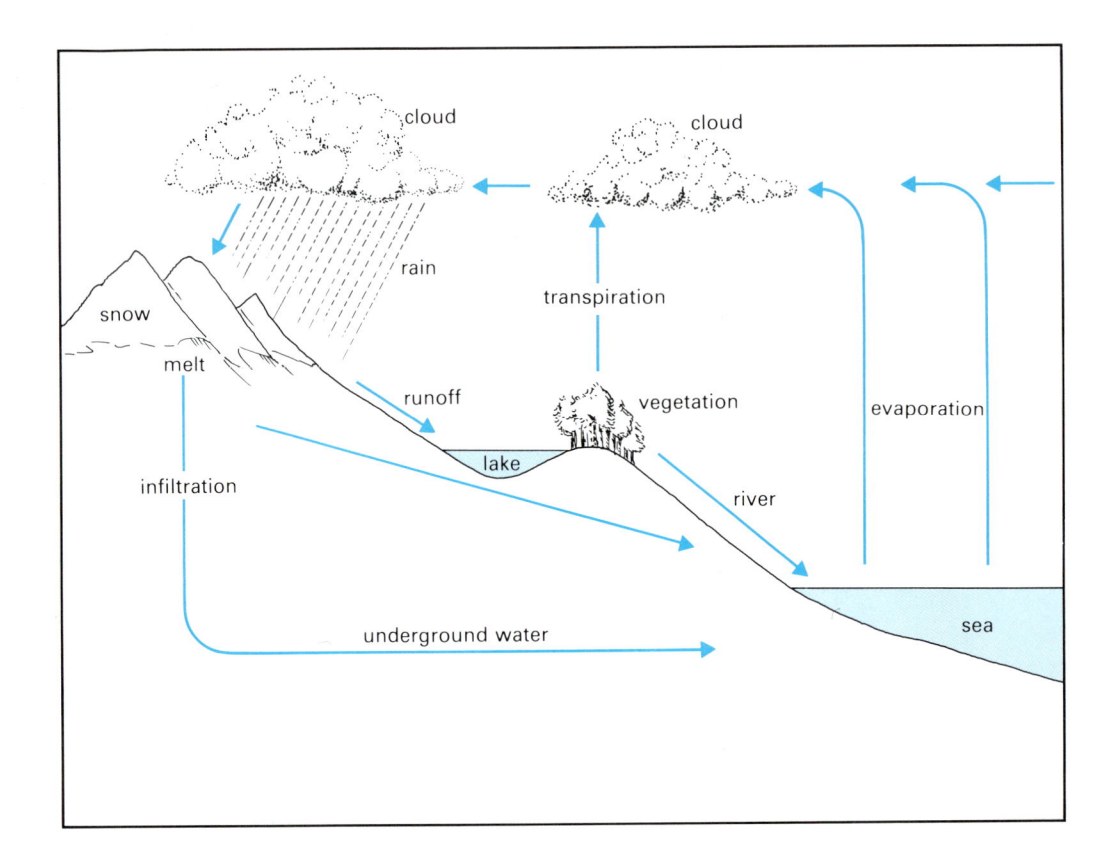

Fig. 96 A river basin.

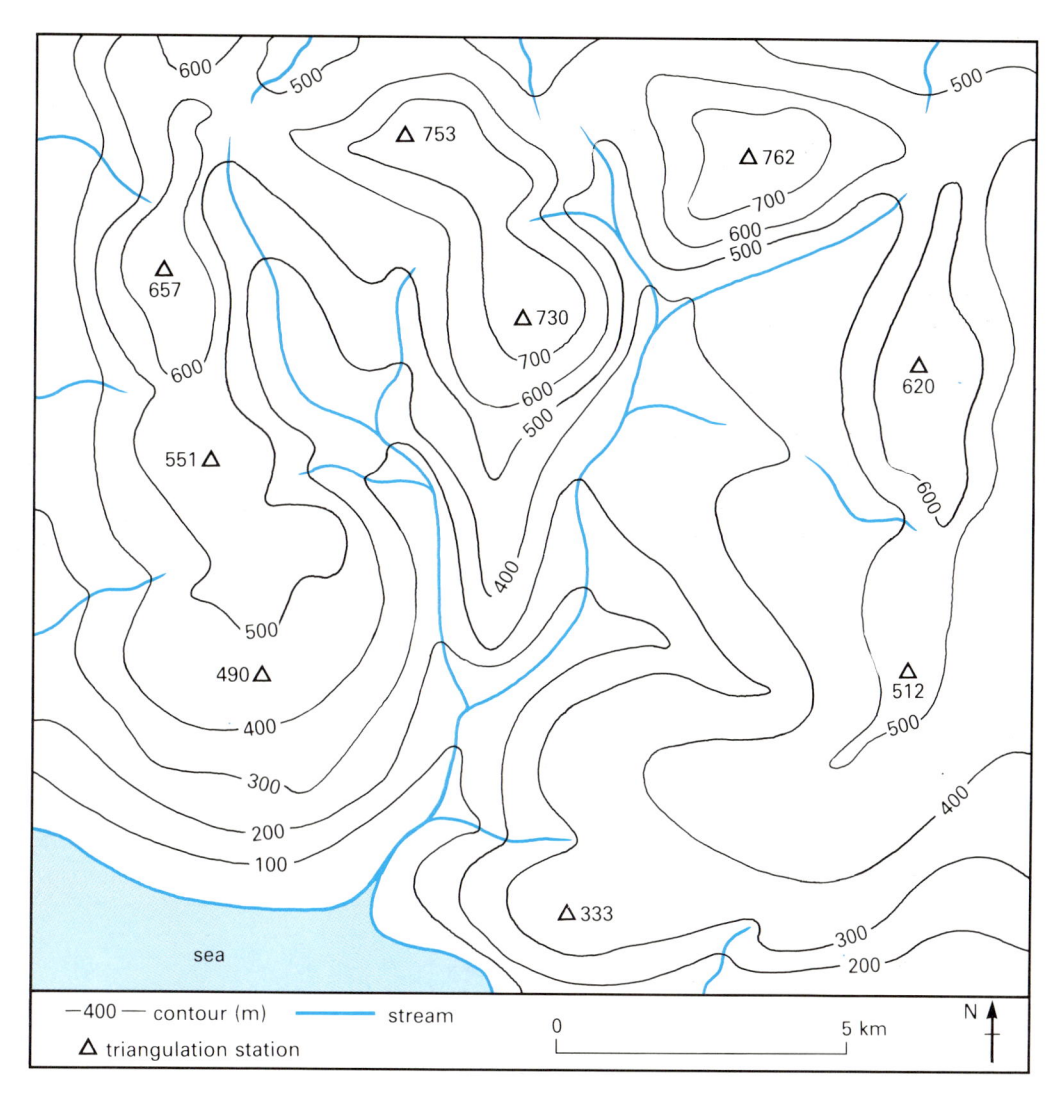

Fig. 97 Slapton River, Devon – rainfall and discharge.

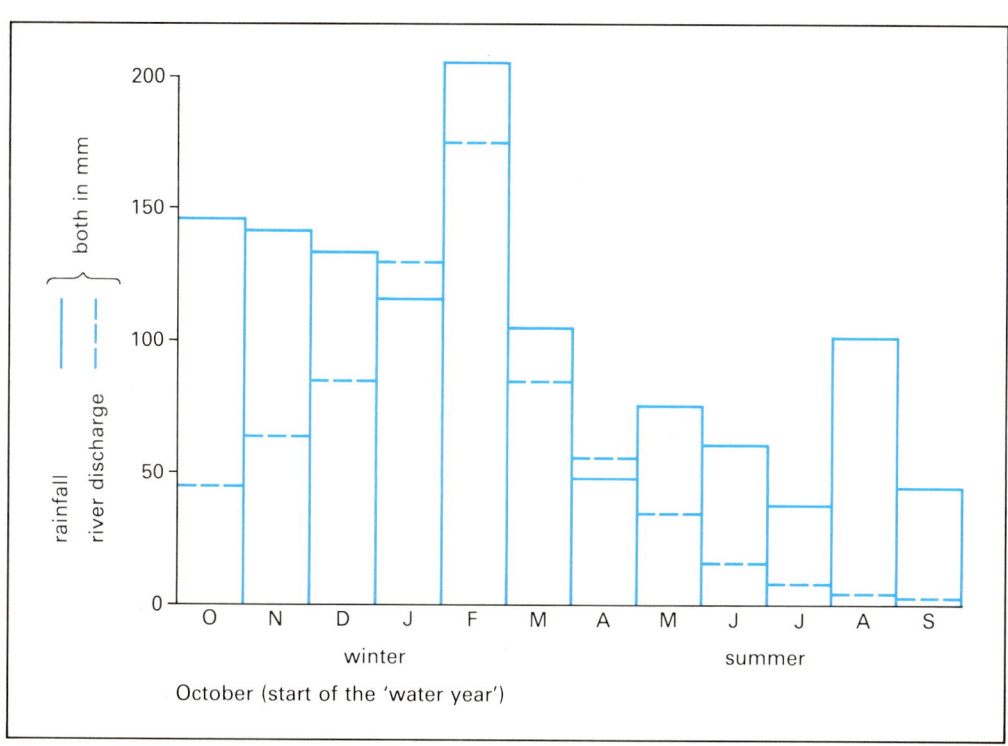

Water deficits

Surplus or deficit balances can be very significant to man since rivers form a major source of water for domestic, agricultural and industrial purposes.

The following figures are taken from the Yorkshire Water Authority area (Fig. 98). The forecast figures indicate a major deficit by the end of the century. The response to this type of problem is normally to store water by building new dams and reservoirs.

million litres daily	1971	2001
total demand	1280	2440
total supply	1400	1600
balance	+120	−840

Fig. 98 Yorkshire Water Authority area forecasts.

8 Using Fig. 96 and your tracing overlay, site a dam and reservoir. Try using a dam of maximum height 50 metres. You can then attempt to calculate the surface area of the lake in square kilometres. If you feel really energetic you could use a calculator to work out the possible contribution of this reservoir to the needs of the Yorkshire Water Authority.

Reservoirs bring great advantages, but they can be a source of major disasters – as Fig. 99 shows.

Systems analysis is one method of analysing both the hydrological cycle and its benefits and dangers. This kind of analysis may be familiar to you if you know how to program a computer, and it has widespread use in geography. Fig. 100 shows some of the main symbols and terms used in systems diagrams.

9 Produce a simple systems diagram to describe the process of cleaning your teeth.

Fig. 101 shows a far more complex systems diagram which summarises a small part of the hydrological cycle. It explains the relationship between part of the natural cycle and people's need for water in towns and industry. The regulators are not all labelled.

10 Identify and label the regulators (or switches) in Fig. 101 which would be important in preventing flood disasters like that in Fig. 99.
11 Redraw sub-system B on Fig. 101 to take into account some of the problems faced by the Yorkshire Water Authority in 2001 (Fig. 98).

Fig. 99 A dam disaster.

Village is buried in day of disaster

THE *GUARDIAN*, 20 July 1985

From George Armstrong in Rome

Two hundred and sixty people were feared dead last night after a dam burst in the Italian Dolomites, washing away three crowded hotels and 20 holiday chalets in the tourist resort of Stava, near Calavese. A 2½-mile river of mud and rubble marks the disaster scene.

Rescue workers believed few people could have survived the onslaught of the 150ft wide wall of water, mud and mountain debris, said to have reached 120ft high at some points.

The Civil Protection Ministry estimated that the earth-work dam released some 250,000 cubic metres of water in 20 seconds. Fifty boy scouts from Milan were at first believed to be in Stava, but it was later established that they had instead set up camp in Dimaro, a village 28 miles away.

The Civil Protection Minister, Mr Giuseppe Zamberletti, told reporters that 78 bodies had been recovered and 195 people were still unaccounted for.

"It sounded like an earthquake, I thought the mountain had collapsed," one resident told Italian television. Another, who broke down in tears, commented: "I saw the end of the world."

About 120 of those missing were guests in the stricken hotels. Fifteen were holiday makers staying in rented houses and 60 were villagers. Fifteen people had been found alive in the sea of mud and debris, and 15 others had been injured, two of them seriously.

First reports of the disaster suggested that an embankment on the dam, built 20 years ago of earth and boulders to filter waste water from a flourite mine, had given way. The mine and the dam were owned, until 1981, by the state petrochemical agency, ENI. The collapse of the dam wall also released tons of sediment from the mine effluents pumped into the dam.

The area had received unusually heavy and persistent rains in the past few weeks which substantially raised the normal level of the dam, located 4,000ft up in the Trento-Alto Adige resort area. It is much frequented by German and Austrian tourists.

Fig. 100 Systems diagrams – some basic terms.

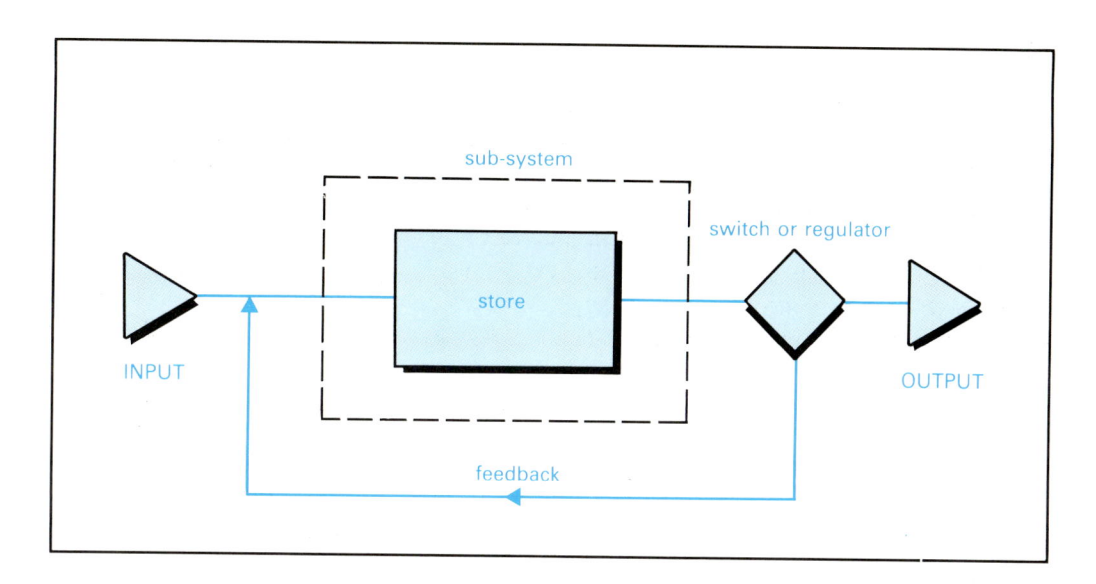

Fig. 101 Part of the water cycle system.

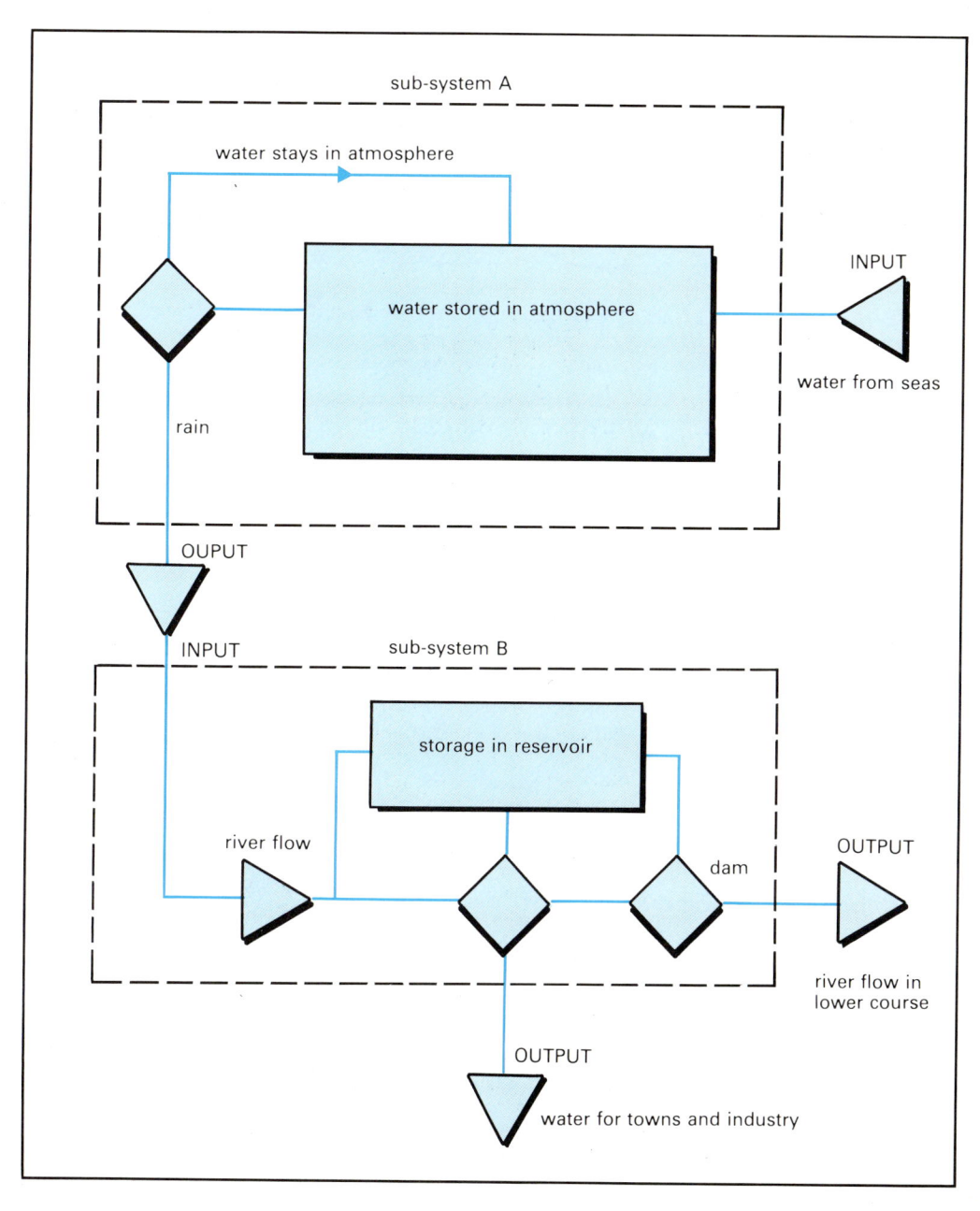

55

Circular diagrams and more systems

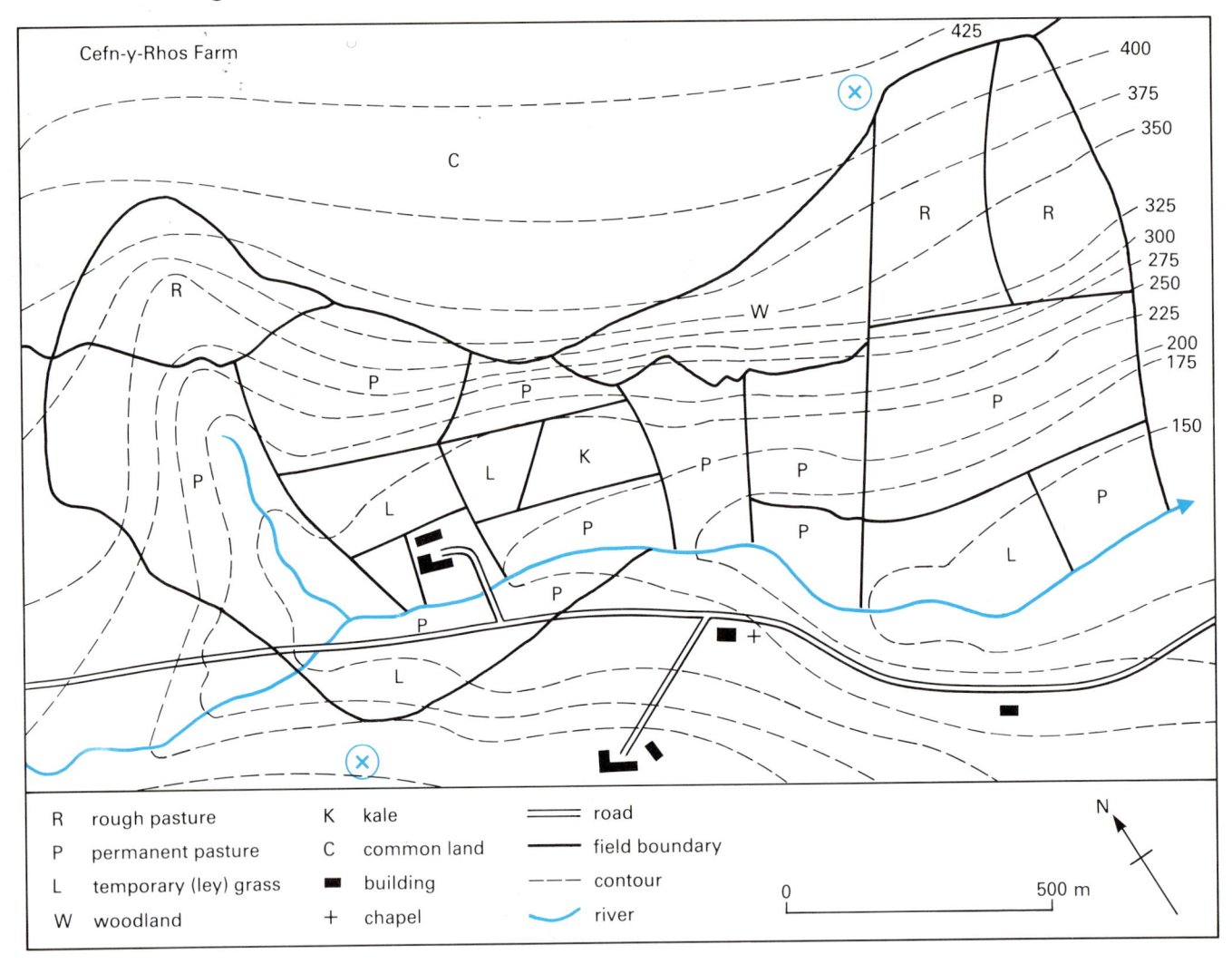

Fig. 102 A Welsh hill farm.

Legend:
- R rough pasture
- P permanent pasture
- L temporary (ley) grass
- W woodland
- K kale
- C common land
- building
- + chapel
- road
- field boundary
- contour
- river

Studies of farms are a common method of looking at agriculture. Frequently farms are described using various types of maps and diagrams. The **map of land use** in Fig. 102 shows a Welsh hill farm which is a beef rearing/fattening and sheep enterprise, making use of extensive common land.

1 Using the square counting technique described on page 10 calculate the area of the farm in square metres and then convert to hectares. Ignore the area of common land which is shared with other farms.

2 Draw a cross-section from the map between the two Xs marked on the map. Use the techniques described on page 21, but add on the field boundaries and write in the land use across your section. What is the relationship between land use and slope on this farm?

A further method of describing farming activity is to draw a **circular graph** for 'The year's work'. Fig. 103 is an example for an East Anglian farm of about 200 hectares on rich, fertile, flat land.

3 Write a brief but complete account of the major activities on the farm at different seasons. Does your account explain why this farm is largely mechanised?

A popular method of analysing the complexity of a farm is to make use of systems analysis – similar to that used with the water cycle on pages 54 to 55.

Look at a total **farm system** in Fig. 104. The diagram uses the same basic terms as Fig. 100. It gives a detailed picture of a market garden enterprise in the Vale of Evesham.

4 Using Fig. 104 write a description of how the system works. If you have only limited time pick out one aspect (e.g. Short Term Input) and describe that in detail.

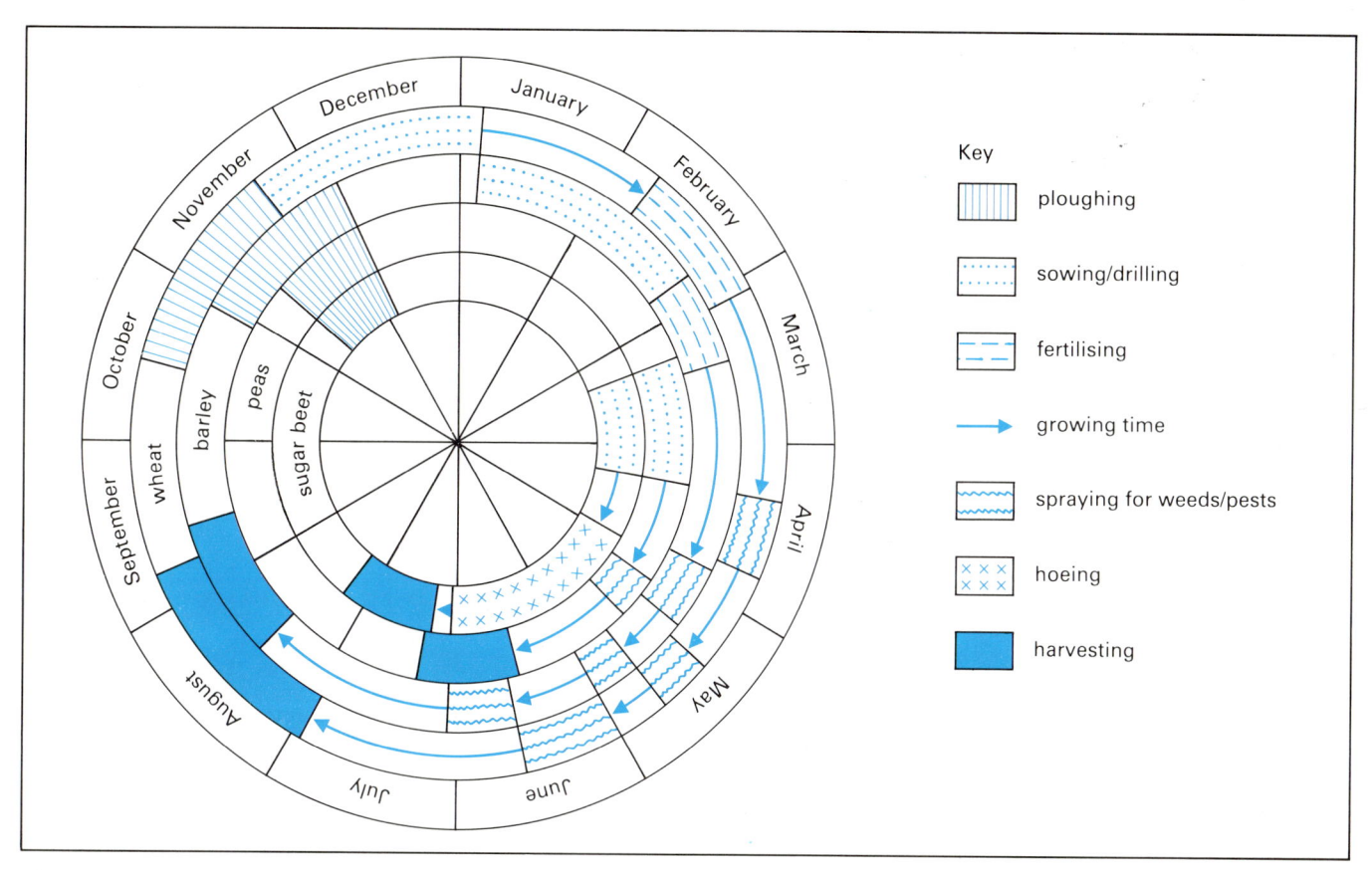

Fig. 103 A year's work on an East Anglian farm.

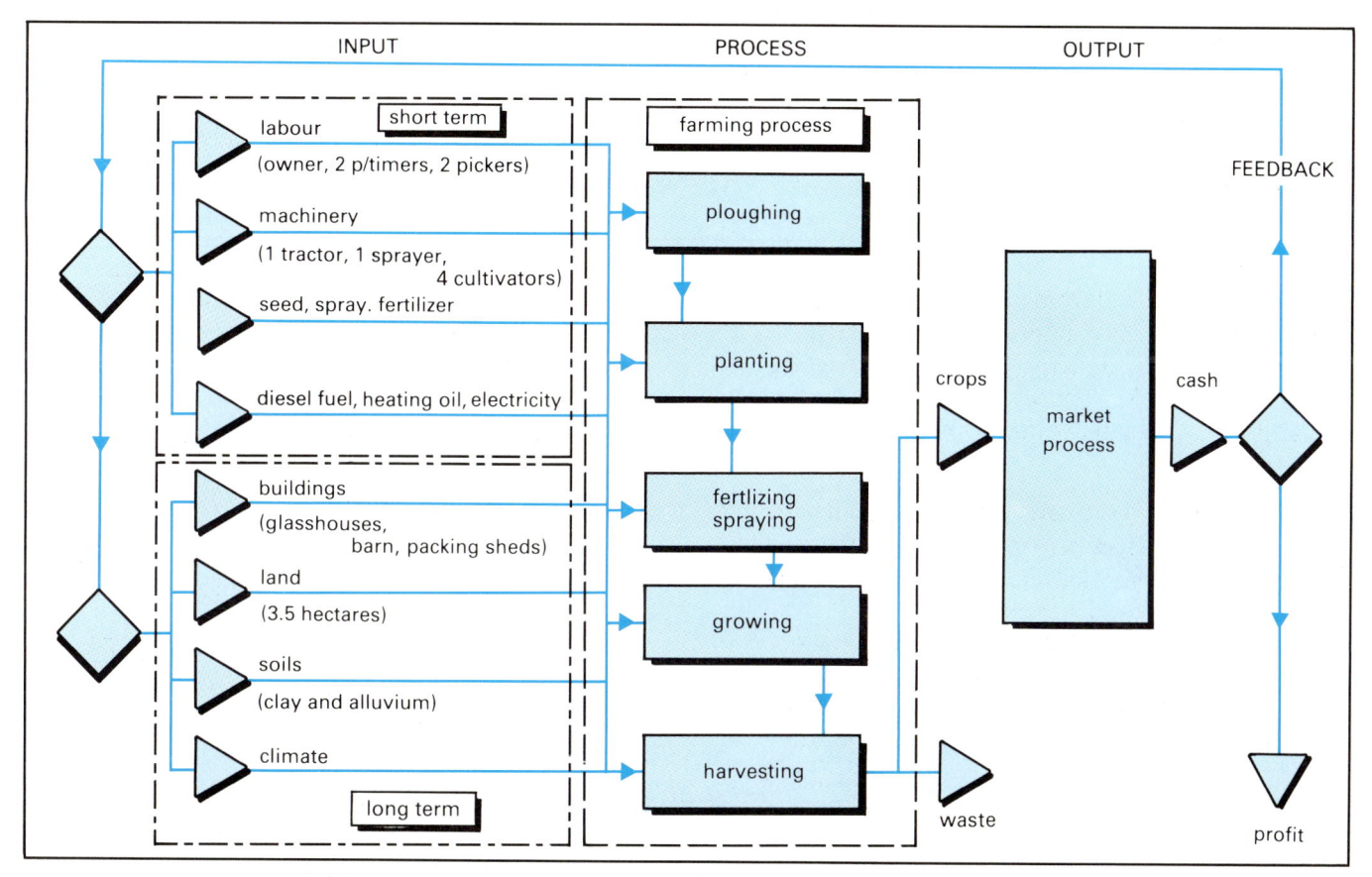

Fig. 104 A farm system based on a market garden in the Vale of Evesham.

Land use maps and sketches

Amenity and conflict

An alternative type of land use map is often used in looking at leisure facilities or amenities. The one-inch tourist map of Dartmoor and the 1:25 000 Outdoor Leisure Maps make use of many of the same techniques as these. Fig. 105 shows one of the most extensive Forestry Commission holdings in Britain.

1 Using Fig. 105 explain in what ways recreation is provided for in the area. Why is there increasing demand for such amenities?

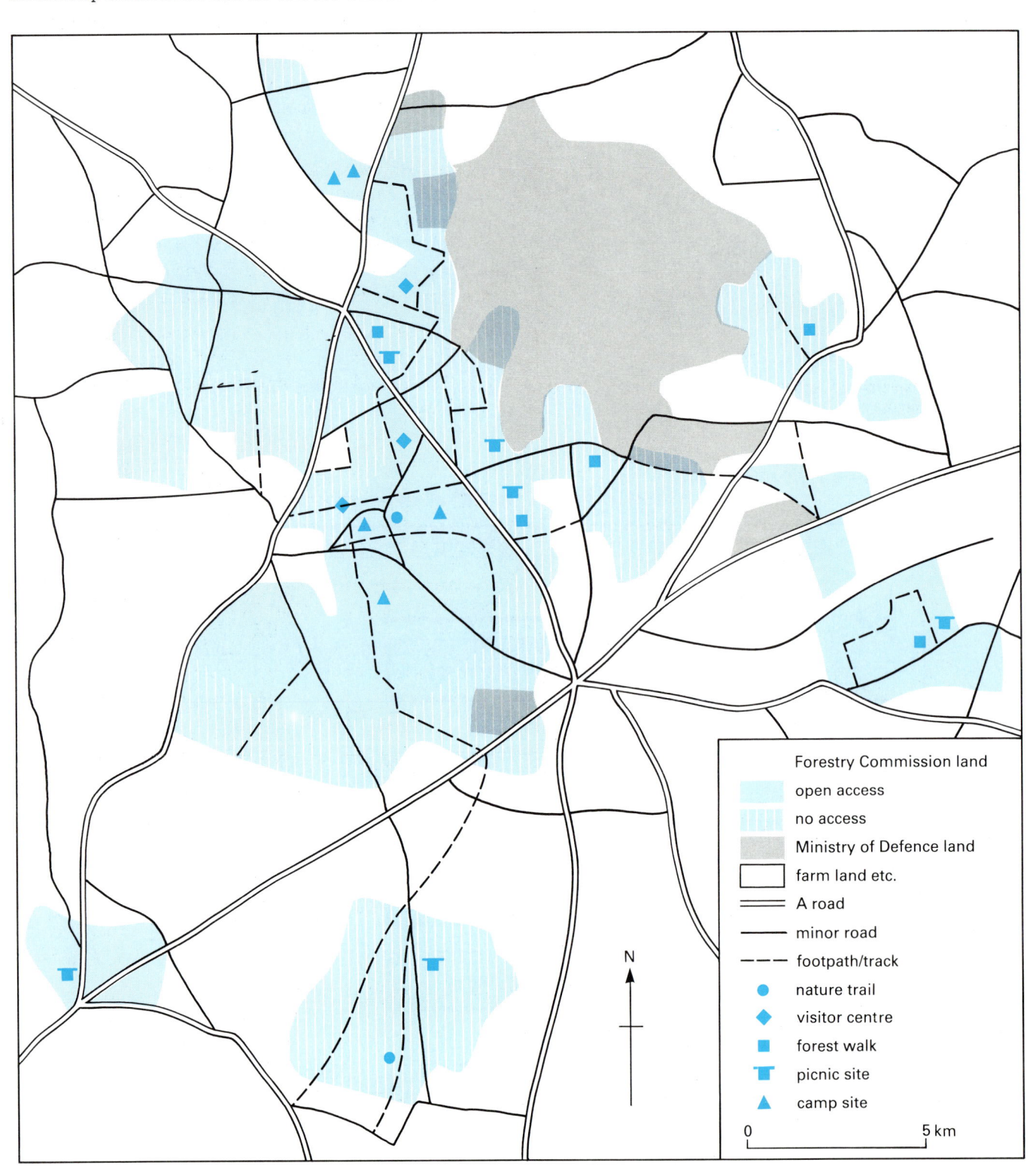

Fig. 105 Thetford Forest, East Anglia.

A difficulty in many parts of the world is **conflicting land use** requirements for the same area of land. The Forestry Commission is clearly trying to accommodate both forestry and recreation in the same area. The **set diagram** Fig. 106 is similar to diagrams used in mathematics. The particular example shows the conflict immediately around the oil refineries at Milford Haven in SW Wales. The diagram could have been extended to include the military training areas south of Milford Haven.

2 Using the information above and Fig. 106, draw a four set diagram to illustrate the land use conflicts in the Thetford area.

Field sketching is frequently used in geography fieldwork as a method of recording. Annotated sketches can include a great deal of information about leisure – and other – facilities in an area. Fig. 107 shows the area of Northam Burrows on the estuary of the Rivers Taw and Torridge on the north Devon coast (Map Extract 9).

3 Using the ideas from the previous exercise list some land use conflicts on Fig. 107. Using an appropriate key, draw a map of the area showing the different types of land use.

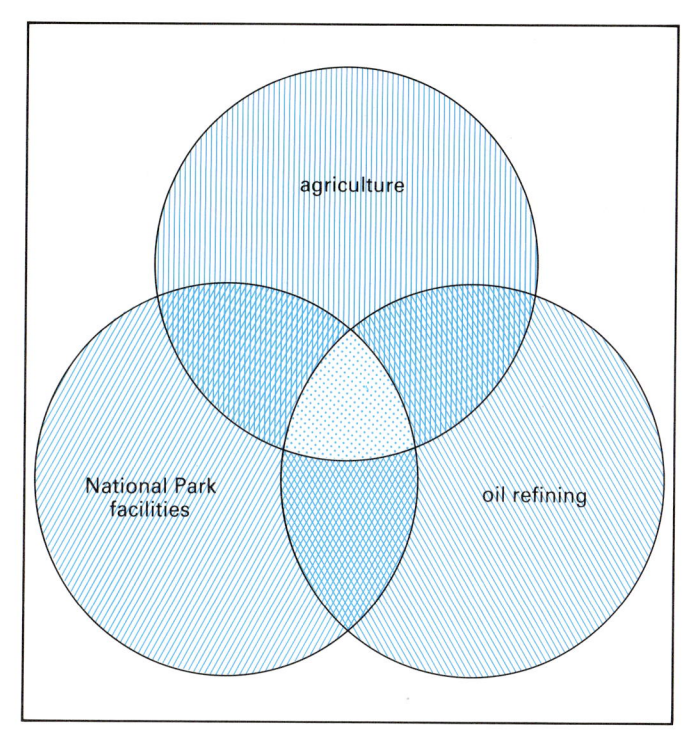

Fig. 106 Land use conflicts in the Pembrokeshire National Park near Milford Haven.

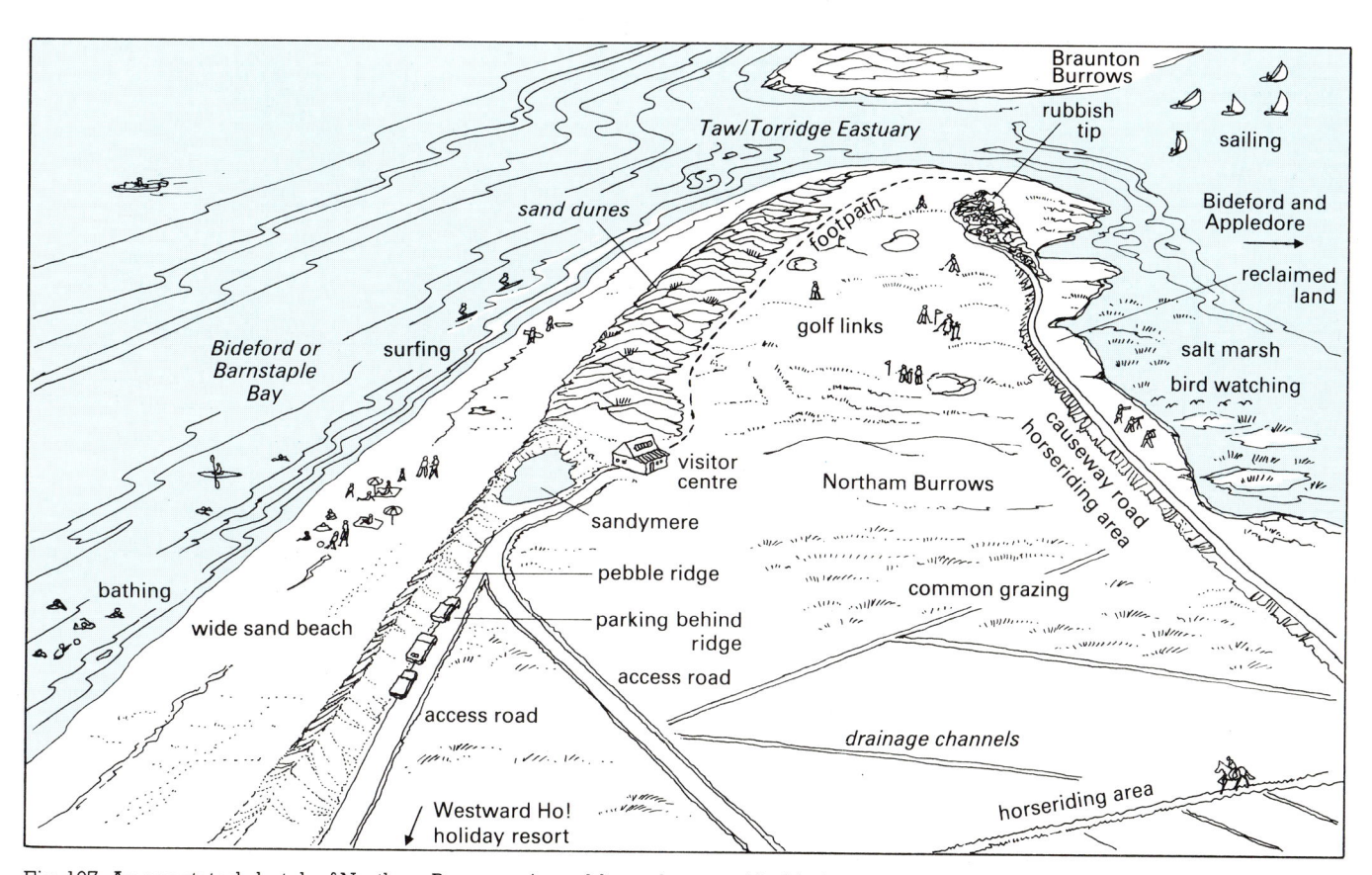

Fig. 107 An annotated sketch of Northam Burrows viewed from above and behind Westward Ho!

Models and zones

Very generalised maps of land use in towns enable us to identify **urban zones** – that is, areas where one type of land use is dominant. Fig. 108 shows the three main types of urban land use in zones for the twin towns of Warwick and Royal Leamington Spa. The three zones normally identified are **residential**, **industrial** and **services**. In the case of the last they are shown on this map as the Central Business Districts (CBD) and the neighbourhood shopping centres.

1. Study Fig. 109 which shows a very generalised **model** of a British town – you may have seen three or four different models based on different principles. Now attempt a generalised model of Warwick or Leamington based on a circular segmented grid. Does it bear any relationship to the model in Fig. 109?

A planned New Town

Modern town planners are keen on keeping different types of land use apart – for example they do not like industry developing in the middle of residential areas. This need to keep different functions separate is seen most clearly in the planned functional zones of New Towns.

Fig. 110 shows Washington New Town. Compare it with Fig. 108 of Warwick and Leamington (notice the scales of the maps). Its planned population is 80 000 but by 1986 it was still well below the total for Warwick and Leamington together.

2. What is the most striking difference between Fig. 108 and Fig. 110?
3. Using Map Extract 6 identify the housing estates lettered A–J on Fig. 110.
4. What are the advantages and disadvantages of (a) living in a New Town (b) setting up industry in a New Town? Use the advertisements in Fig. 111 to answer (b).

Fig. 108 The major urban zones of Warwick (pop. 20 000) and Royal Leamington Spa (pop. 40 000).

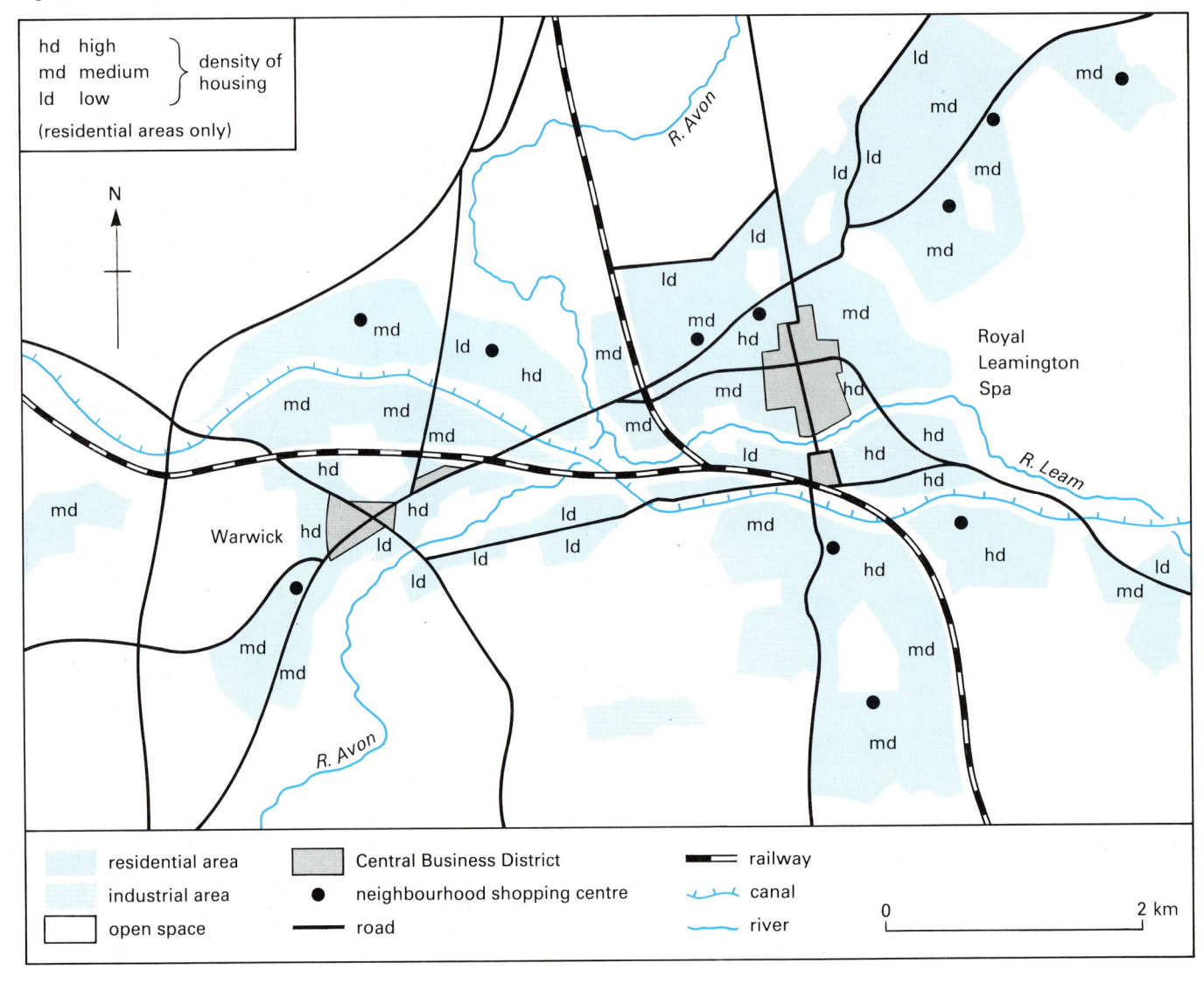

Fig. 109 Model of functional zones in British towns.

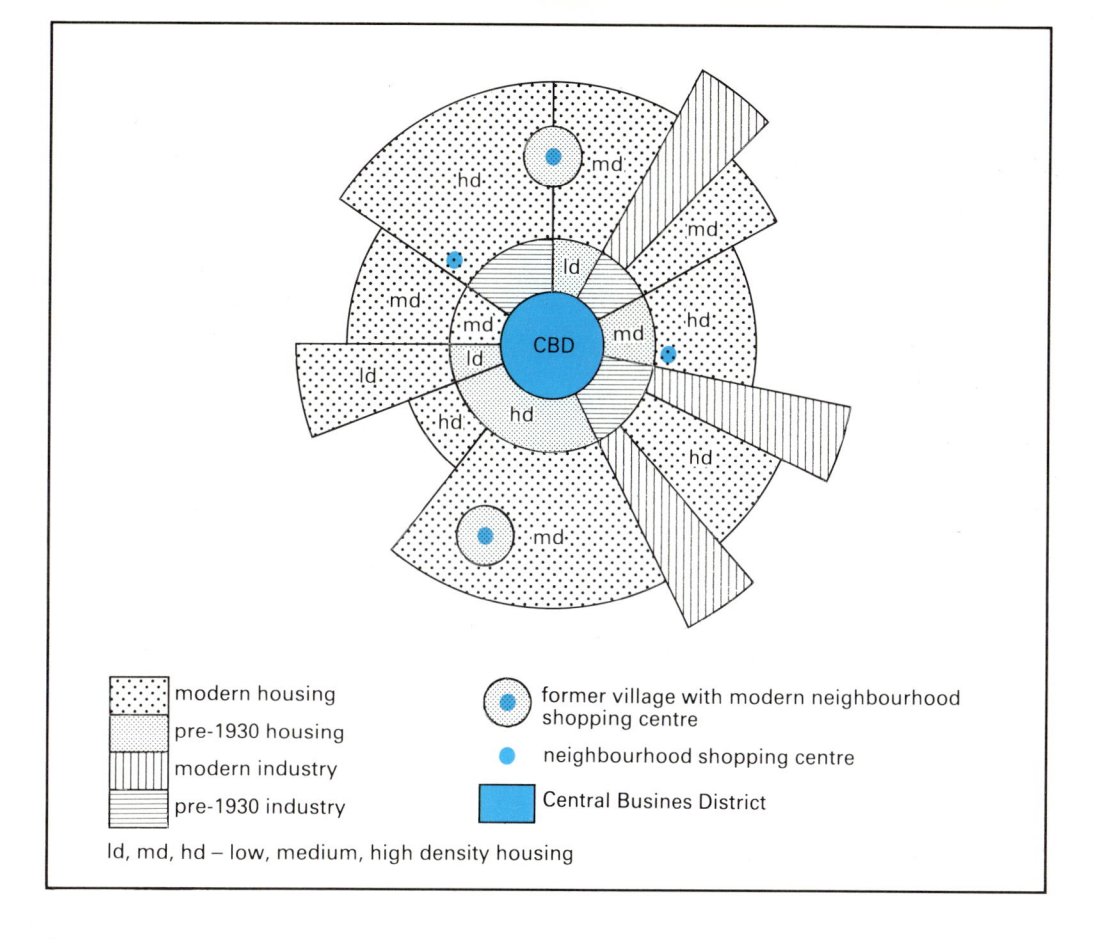

- modern housing
- pre-1930 housing
- modern industry
- pre-1930 industry
- former village with modern neighbourhood shopping centre
- neighbourhood shopping centre
- Central Busines District

ld, md, hd – low, medium, high density housing

Fig. 110 Washington New Town – functional zones.

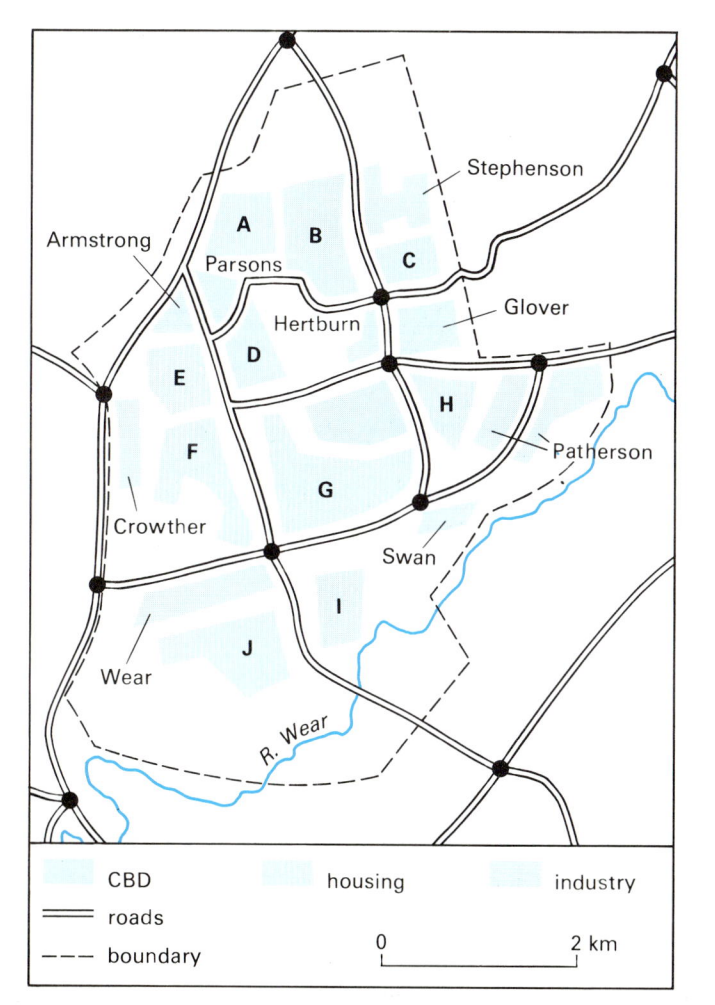

Fig. 111 Advertisements for Washington and Swindon.

Come site-seeing in Washington

It's closer than you think. In the North East of England in fact, where we're helping the tiny settlement that was the world's first Washington to grow into one of Britain's best new towns. One of our jobs is to attract industry to the North East – and since we've helped over 160 companies to relocate here in the last 10 years, we've had plenty of practice – both in giving advice and coping with the practical problems of relocation. Our team of experts offer the industrialist a comprehensive and efficient service from the initial enquiry to final move (and afterwards). Advance factories from 15000 sq ft upwards are available now ... we can give advice on grants and incentives (we're in a Special Development Area) ... the area has an abundant skilled labour supply ... all this and much more, since its all within the framework of a thriving new town.

We need more space than this to tell you about Washington ... why not come and see for yourself what we've got to offer? – Its more than a greenfield site – and the A1(M) goes through the town.

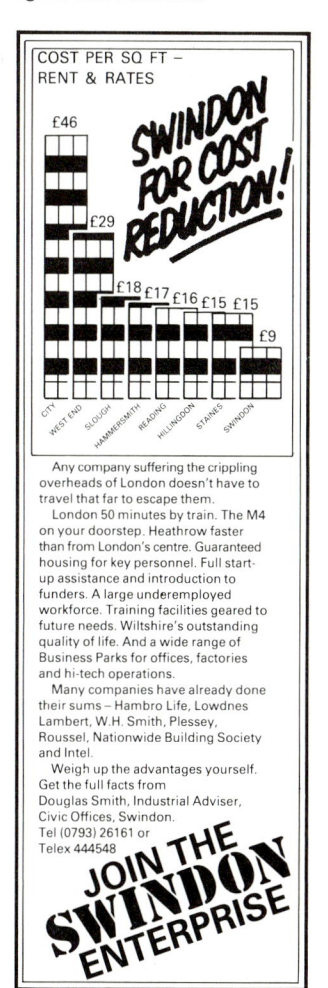

SWINDON FOR COST REDUCTION!

COST PER SQ FT – RENT & RATES

£46 CITY, £29 WEST END, £18 SLOUGH, £17 READING, £16 HAMMERSMITH, £15 HILLINGDON, £15 STAINES, £9 SWINDON

Any company suffering the crippling overheads of London doesn't have to travel that far to escape them.

London 50 minutes by train. The M4 on your doorstep. Heathrow faster than from London's centre. Guaranteed housing for key personnel. Full start-up assistance and introduction to funders. A large underemployed workforce. Training facilities geared to future needs. Wiltshire's outstanding quality of life. And a wide range of Business Parks for offices, factories and hi-tech operations.

Many companies have already done their sums – Hambro Life, Lowdnes Lambert, W.H. Smith, Plessey, Roussel, Nationwide Building Society and Intel.

Weigh up the advantages yourself. Get the full facts from Douglas Smith, Industrial Adviser, Civic Offices, Swindon. Tel (0793) 26161 or Telex 444548

JOIN THE SWINDON ENTERPRISE

Maps and pictures

Fig. 112 Village change – Buriton 1841–1973.

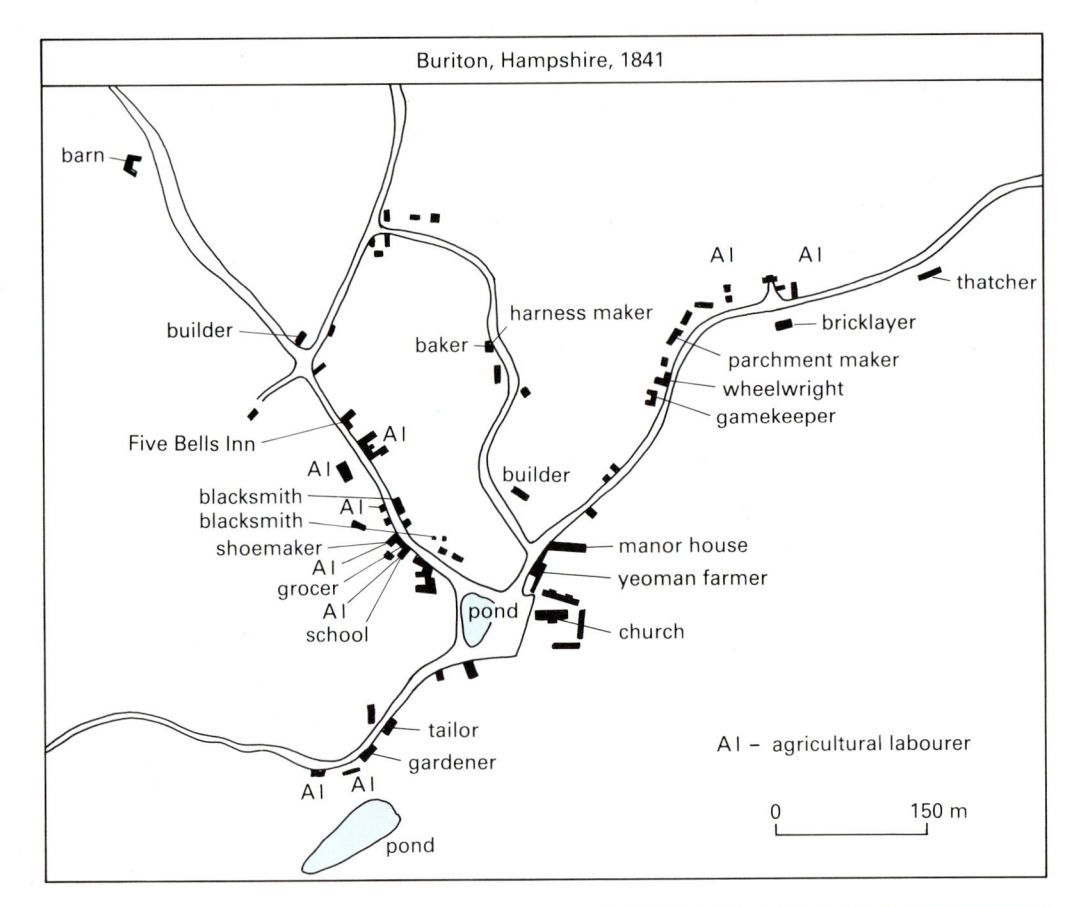

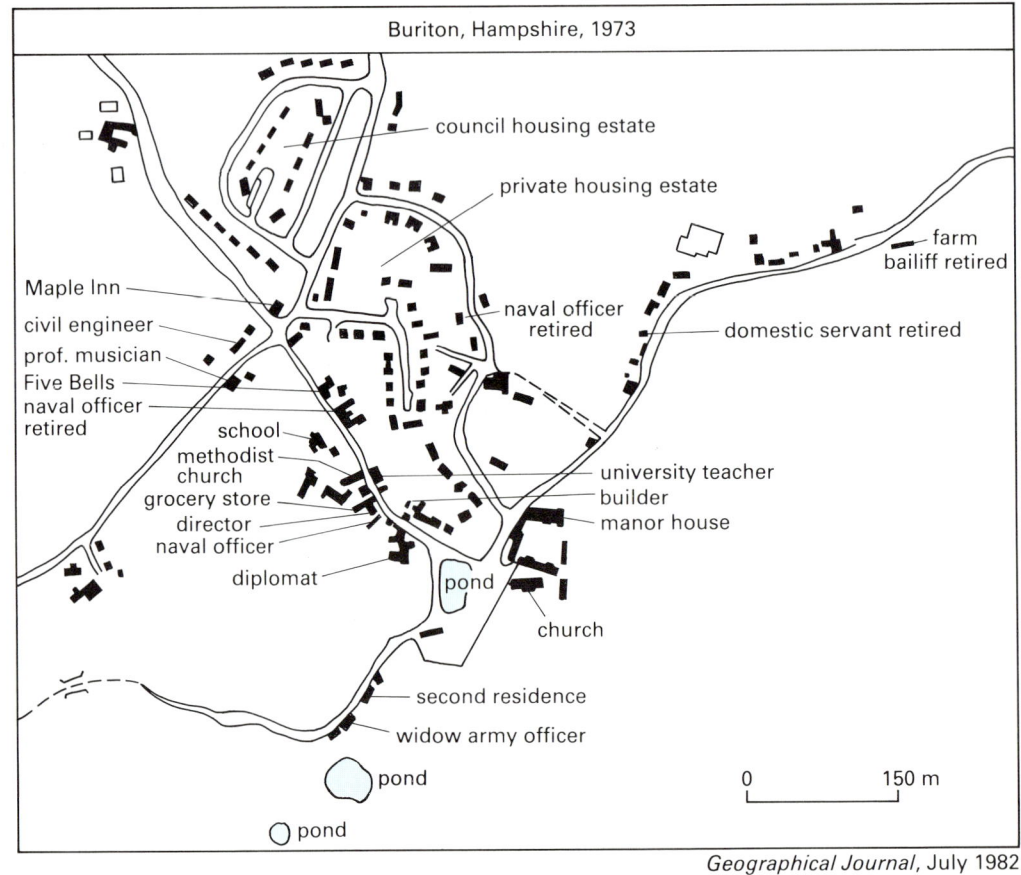

Geographical Journal, July 1982

Changes in time and space

Towns and villages change considerably through time, and they also differ within from area to area. The two maps in Fig. 112 show the village of Buriton, which is about 24 km (15 miles) north of Portsmouth, for the years 1841 and 1973.

1 Clearly the village has changed considerably between these dates. Write notes on the changes that have occurred, using the following titles:
   (a) Road layout and buildings.
   (b) Shops and services (of all types).
   (c) Occupations – but note that the 1973 map is far from complete.

Urban areas show similar changes as the two extracts in Fig. 113 show for a northern town between 1850 and 1950.

2 Describe the changes from 1850–1950 in Fig. 113 with regard to road layout and buildings.

Fig. 113 Town change – 1850–1950.

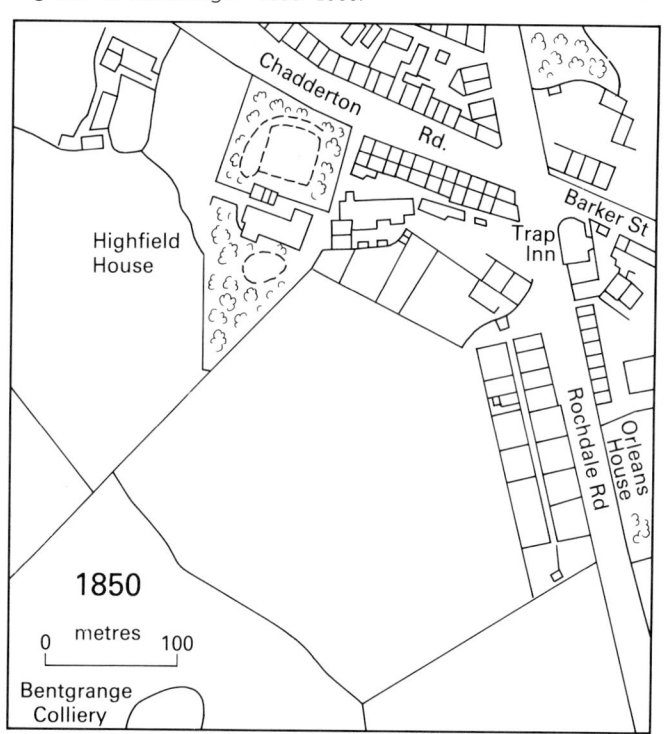

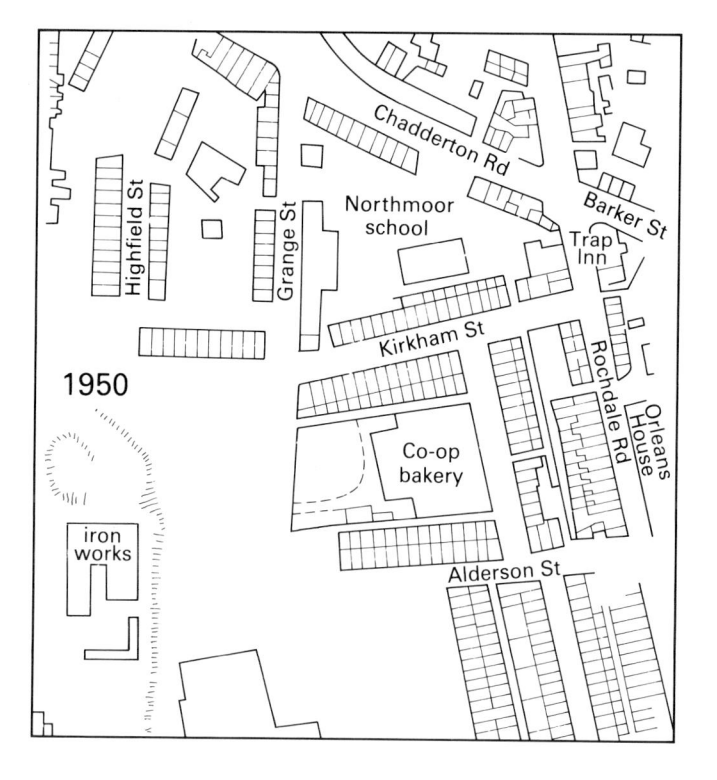

Houses and history

Fig. 114 Three types of housing – A, B and C.

"Wave bye bye to Gran!"

Differences occur in space as well as in time. Such differences are easily shown up by photographs and maps of different **types of houses** in the same area. These differences are often a reflection of the time at which they were built.

1. What kind of housing are A, B and C in Fig. 114?
2. Fit the photographs and pictures A, B and C in Fig. 114 to the correct maps from the selection I, II, III, IV in Fig. 115.
3. Using Map Extracts 2 and 6, for each extract find an area of housing similar to maps I–IV in Fig. 115. Remember that the scales are different!

Fig. 115 Maps of four different areas of housing. Each area is 100 m by 100 m.

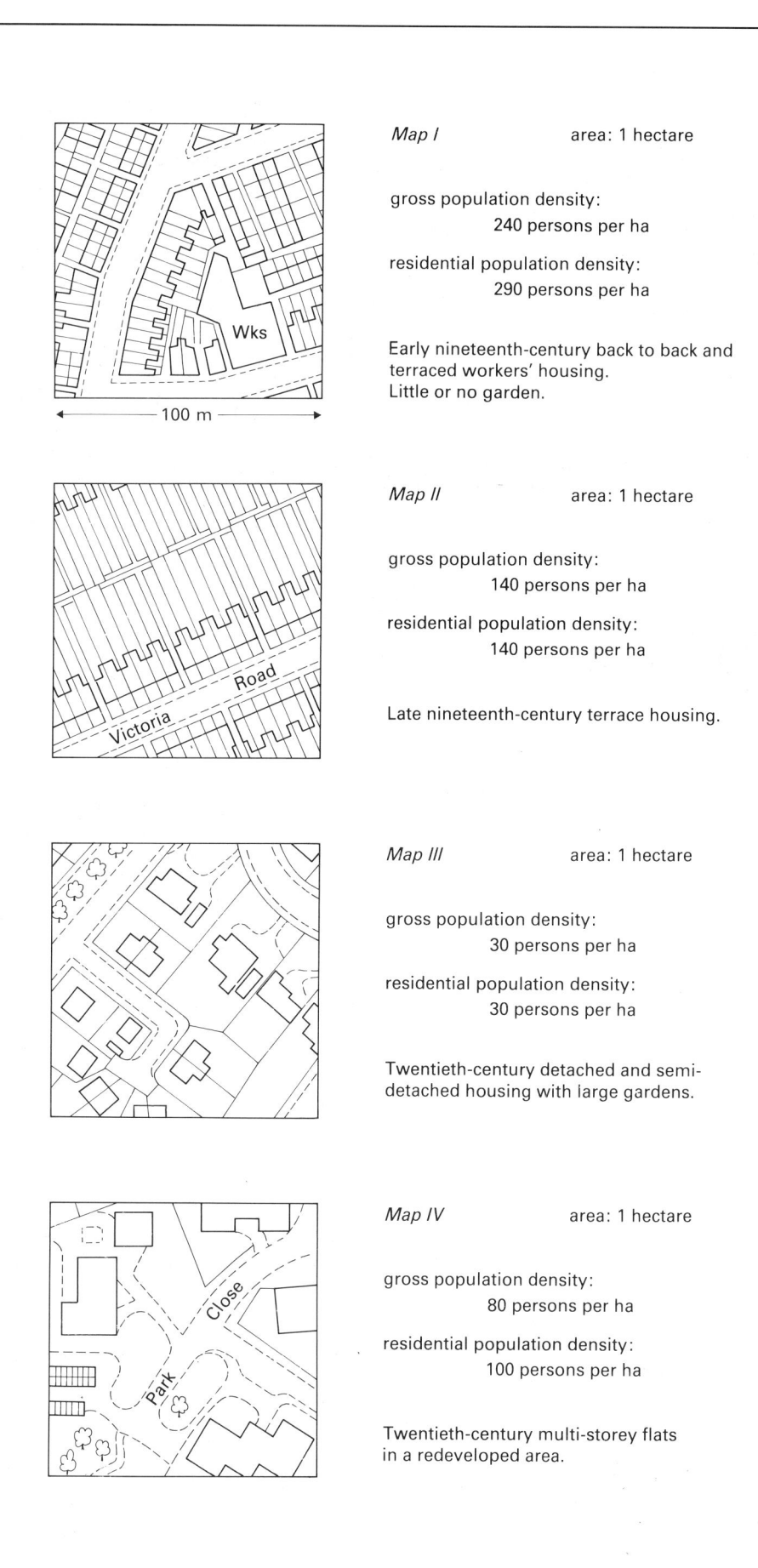

Map I area: 1 hectare

gross population density:
 240 persons per ha

residential population density:
 290 persons per ha

Early nineteenth-century back to back and terraced workers' housing. Little or no garden.

Map II area: 1 hectare

gross population density:
 140 persons per ha

residential population density:
 140 persons per ha

Late nineteenth-century terrace housing.

Map III area: 1 hectare

gross population density:
 30 persons per ha

residential population density:
 30 persons per ha

Twentieth-century detached and semi-detached housing with large gardens.

Map IV area: 1 hectare

gross population density:
 80 persons per ha

residential population density:
 100 persons per ha

Twentieth-century multi-storey flats in a redeveloped area.

Density and dots

Population distribution maps

It is important to understand the pattern of villages and towns across an entire area as well as their internal structure. The spread of **rural settlement** is demonstrated in this section, based on part of Map Extract 15 bounded by eastings 80 and 89 and northings 06 and 13. A glance at the extract shows two small towns and a variety of villages. The population statistics in Fig. 116 show some rather startling contrasts.

1. In Fig. 116 population density for Wickham Bishops gives 276.3 persons per square kilometre. Why is this a rather unsatisfactory statistic?
2. The population density figures for Little Totham and Goldhanger have not been calculated. What are they?

Although density statistics for populations are not very satisfactory because they obscure local variations in distribution, they are very widely used. Fig. 117 shows the statistics on Fig. 116 translated into map form. The shading pattern which becomes denser with the population is generally referred to as **density shading**. Occasionally you will see the maps referred to as **choropleth maps**.

3. Fig. 117 makes use of a geometrical progression. The most widely used geometrical progression for population is 0–64, 64–128, 128–256, 256–512, 512–? Can you calculate the next figure? Now trace the parish boundaries from Fig. 117 and shade in according to this new grouping.
4. A further method of grouping is to use simple arithmetic progression e.g. 0–50, 50–100, 100–150, 150–200, etc. What would be the difficulty with this pattern for the statistics in Fig. 116?

The other popular method of showing population patterns is the **dot map**. While density maps deal with averages, dot maps represent actual amounts. Each dot has a specific value. Fig. 118 shows a dot map of population in the same part of Essex as discussed above. Each dot here has been given a value of 150 persons and

Parish	Population 1981	Area sq kms	Population density per sq km
Witham	25,434	32.5	782.6
Hatfield Peverel	3,946	20.0	47.3
Wickham Bishops	1,934	7.0	276.3
Great Totham	2,675	16.0	167.2
Tolleshunt Major	506	9.5	53.3
Little Totham	410	6.5	
Ulting	129	4.0	32.3
Langford	136	4.0	34.0
Woodham Walter	613	10.0	61.3
Maldon	15,250	21.5	709.3
Goldhanger	579	8.0	

Fig. 116 Population statistics for part of Essex.

then the population for each parish has been represented in dots.

5. What is unsatisfactory about the number of dots in relation to population in Ulting and Langford?
6. Eight dots appear on the part of Witham parish on the map. How many dots should represent the Witham population altogether? Why are there only eight on this map?

The decision about the value of each dot is obviously very difficult when populations of areas are widely different, as they are on this map.

7. Most of the areas of Wickham Bishops, Great Totham, Ulting and Langford are on the map. Trace their outlines and experiment with different dot values. Remember to space the dots evenly over the parish.
8. Although it is usual to space dots evenly there are good reasons for grouping dots. What are they? Now retrace the map and try grouping dots for your four parishes.

Key

☐	under 50
▨	50–99
▦	100–199
▩	200–399
■	over 400

persons per square kilometre

Fig. 117 Population density map for part of Essex.

Fig. 118 Population dot map for part of Essex.

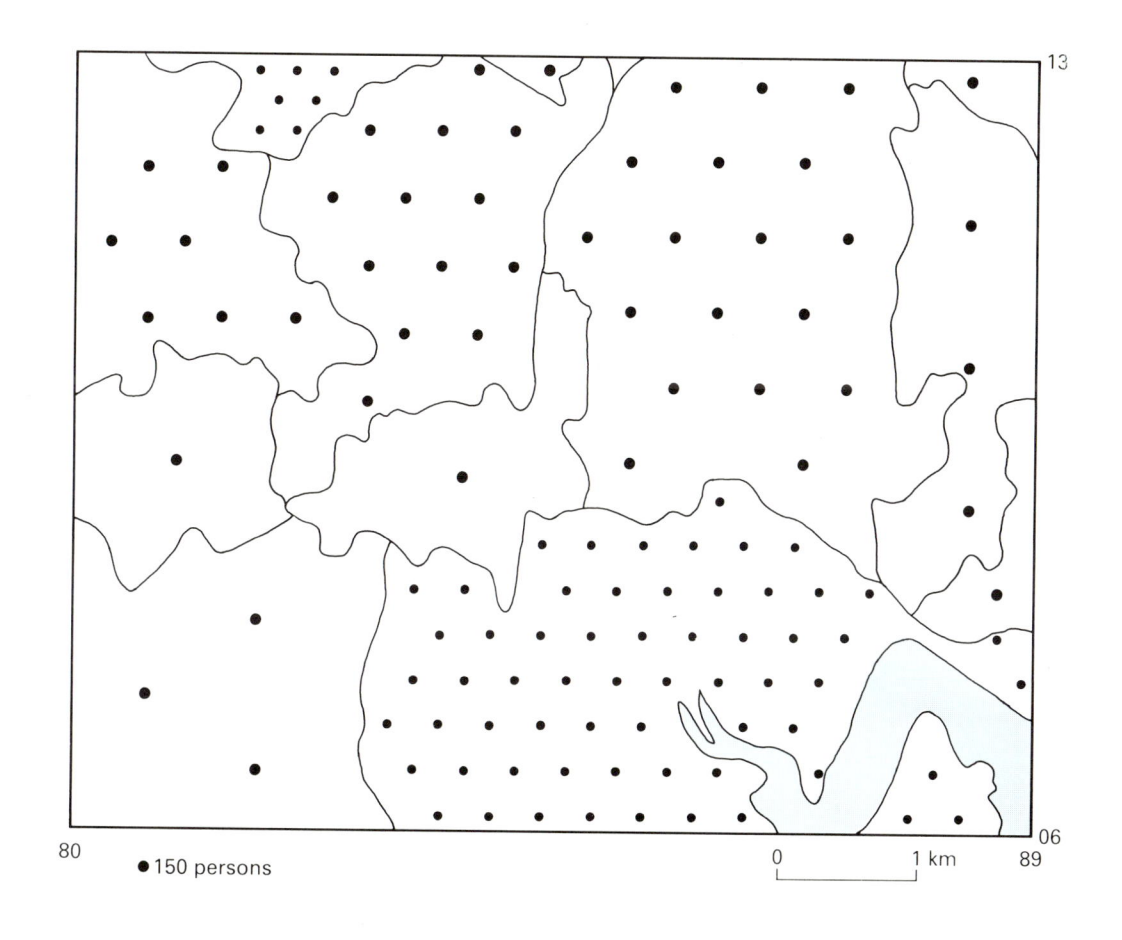

• 150 persons

Circles and pyramids

More on population size

In the last section it became increasingly clear that showing distributions on maps is not easy. The examples all came from population statistics.

There is another method which attempts to show the size of a population, and that is to draw **circles** (or sometimes other shapes) which are **proportional** to the size of populations. Basically the technique uses the area of the circle to relate to the size of population. You may remember that the area of a circle is πr^2. Since π is a constant you actually have to make the population size proportional to the radius squared. Fig. 119 shows the study area mapped by this technique.

1 Without looking back to the statistics, can you work out the actual population for each village?
2 Using the statistics on Fig. 116, what would be the approximate radius of the circles for Hatfield Peverel and Little Totham? You would be best working this out on the key, but some of you may care to work it out accurately with a calculator.

Sometimes you will see proportional circles subdivided like the sections of a fruit pie. These proportional divided circles are sometimes referred to as **pie charts** or **pie diagrams**. Fig. 120 shows proportional divided circles for people working in the Maldon, Essex district in 1981. The larger circle represents 9660 males, the smaller 5200 females and they are divided up into broad categories.

3 Remember that there are 360° in a circle – there are

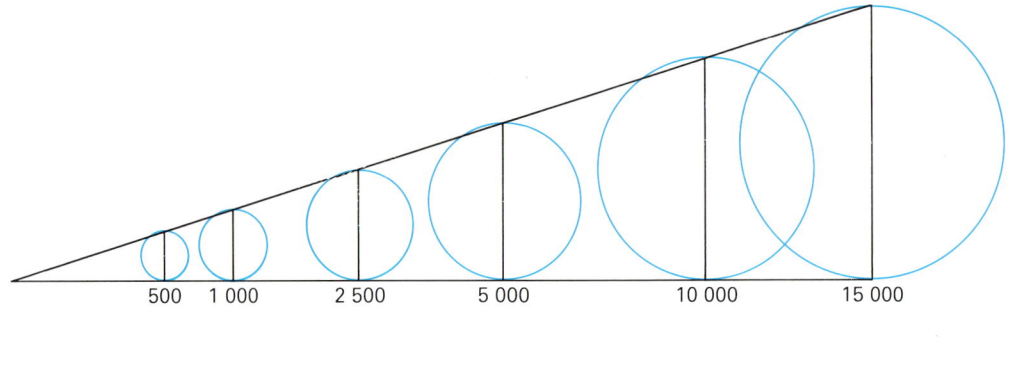

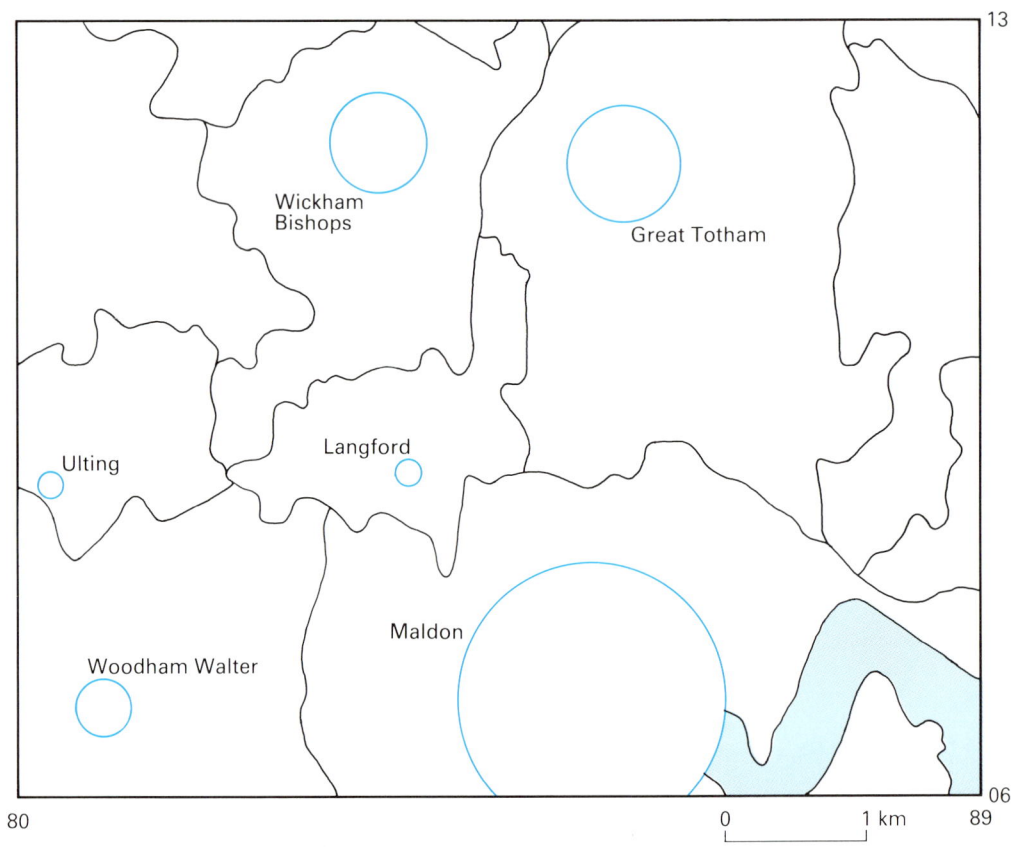

Fig. 119 Population of part of Essex (by parish), proportional circles.

almost 60° of men working in Category I. Can you give this as an actual figure?

4 Now try the same with the 289° of women working in Category IV. You might care to consider whether your home district would provide similar figures.

5 For most of northern and western Britain these Economic Activity Tables in the Census returns hide a major fact about the economy. What is it?

Discussion of population should not only look at spatial distribution, or economic activity but also at age patterns. There are very significant differences between developing and developed countries with regard to age patterns. Normally age patterns are shown by what are called **population pyramids**. A population pyramid for the Maldon district is illustrated in Fig. 121. The total population for the Maldon district in 1981 as shown in the Census was 47 593 persons, of whom 23 579 were males and 24 014 females.

6 Study the population pyramid (fig. 121). How do you think it would compare with a similar diagram for Washington New Town?

7 If the trends in Fig. 121 continue what will be the pattern by the end of the century?

8 Notice the difference in the older age groups between men and women. Using the total figures above, what are the actual numbers of men and women over 64 in the Maldon district?

Fig. 120 People working in Maldon district, 1981.

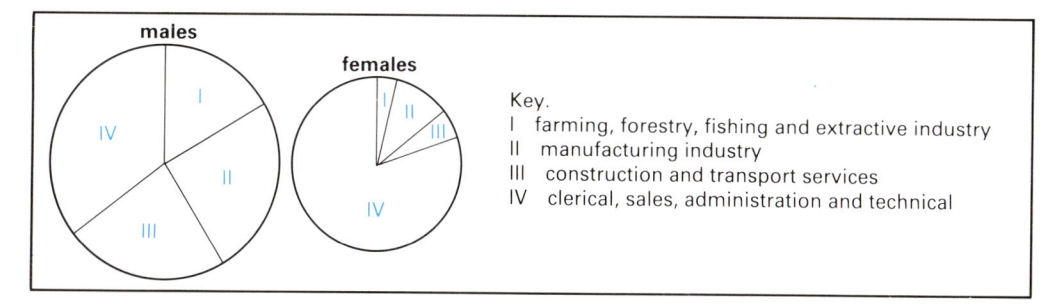

Key.
I farming, forestry, fishing and extractive industry
II manufacturing industry
III construction and transport services
IV clerical, sales, administration and technical

Fig. 121 Population of Maldon district, 1981. Age/sex pyramid.

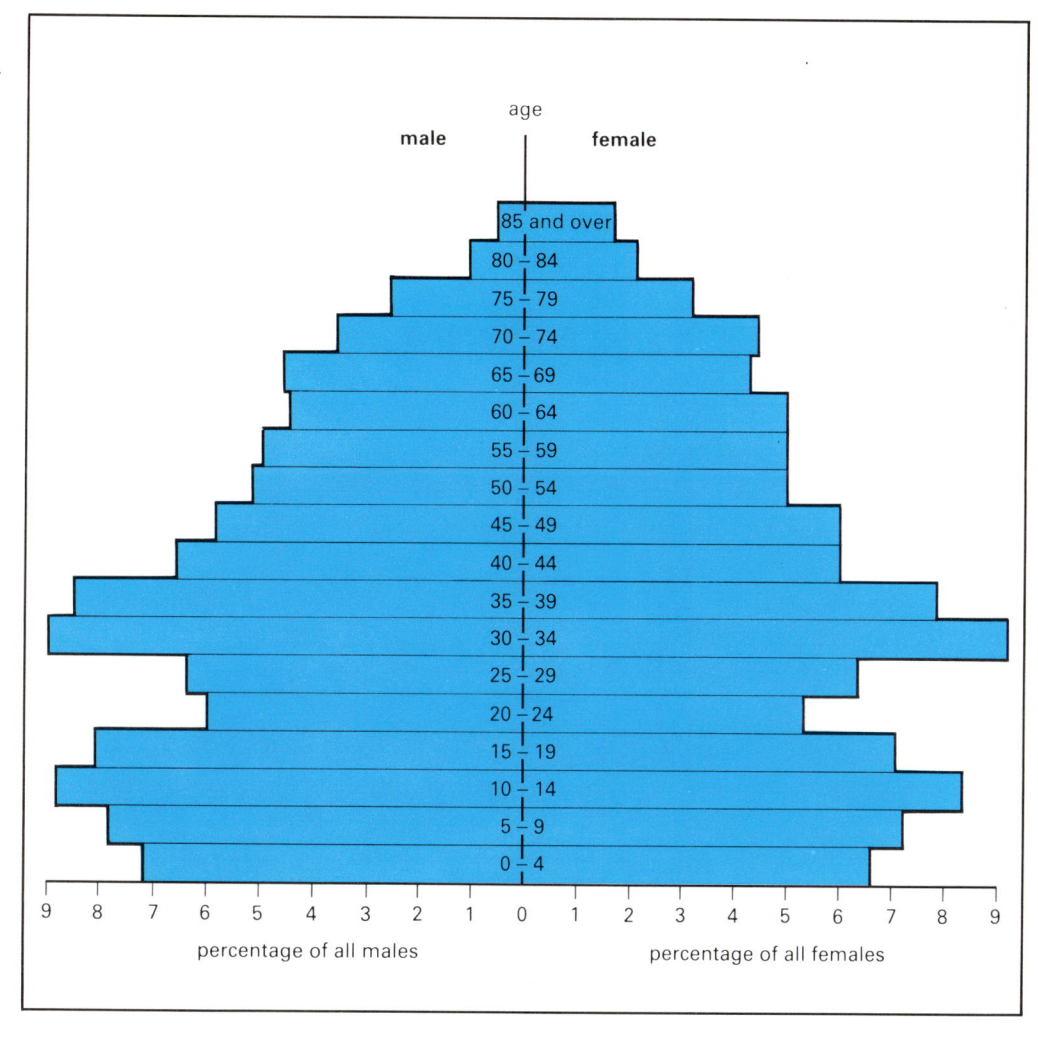

Lines and flows

Let's leave Essex and move down to Devon for the next section. The study area is partly covered by Map Extract 9. You will know that shops tend to be sited in accessible places, and that they tend to cluster together in shopping areas within towns. You may also know that smaller towns have fewer shops than large towns. Fig. 122 shows the relationship between the number of shoe shops and the population of a group of West Country towns. They are actually the towns that attract shoppers for shoes from a small area of north Devon.

1. Why is the population placed on the x axis and the number of shoe shops on the y axis?
2. Although it is not on the graph Penzance, with a population of 20 000, is the biggest town in Cornwall. How many shoe shops is it likely to have on the basis of the graph evidence?
3. Is there a general relationship between population and number of shops?

Fig. 122 shows a type of graph known as a **scattergram**. The smallest town shown is Braunton with a population of about 4 000. Braunton attracts shoppers from a wide area of north Devon. People who shopped in Braunton were interviewed to discover which villages they had come from to buy groceries (there are five grocery shops in Braunton). The survey did not include people who lived and shopped in Braunton, and could not include people who shopped in other villages. Fig. 123 shows the results. The lines on the map are usually referred to as **desire lines**.

4. Why do you think there are no desire lines to the SW of Braunton?
5. The longest line extends for about 7.5 kilometres. How many of the lines are less than half this length? Can you make a general statement about the pattern on the basis of this evidence?

This part of north Devon consists of small farming hamlets and villages with some holiday centres on the coast. The main road system is very much affected by relief. Fig. 124 shows the routes of the main bus services in summer. This type of map is called a **flow map** and shows the daily frequency of buses.

6. Using Fig. 124 estimate the number of buses per day from Braunton to Barnstaple and from Georgham towards Woolacombe. Using Fig. 123 and Fig. 124 do you think the bus service frequency helps to explain the grocery shopping map for Braunton?

Fig. 122 Graph of population and number of shoe shops for a group of West Country towns.

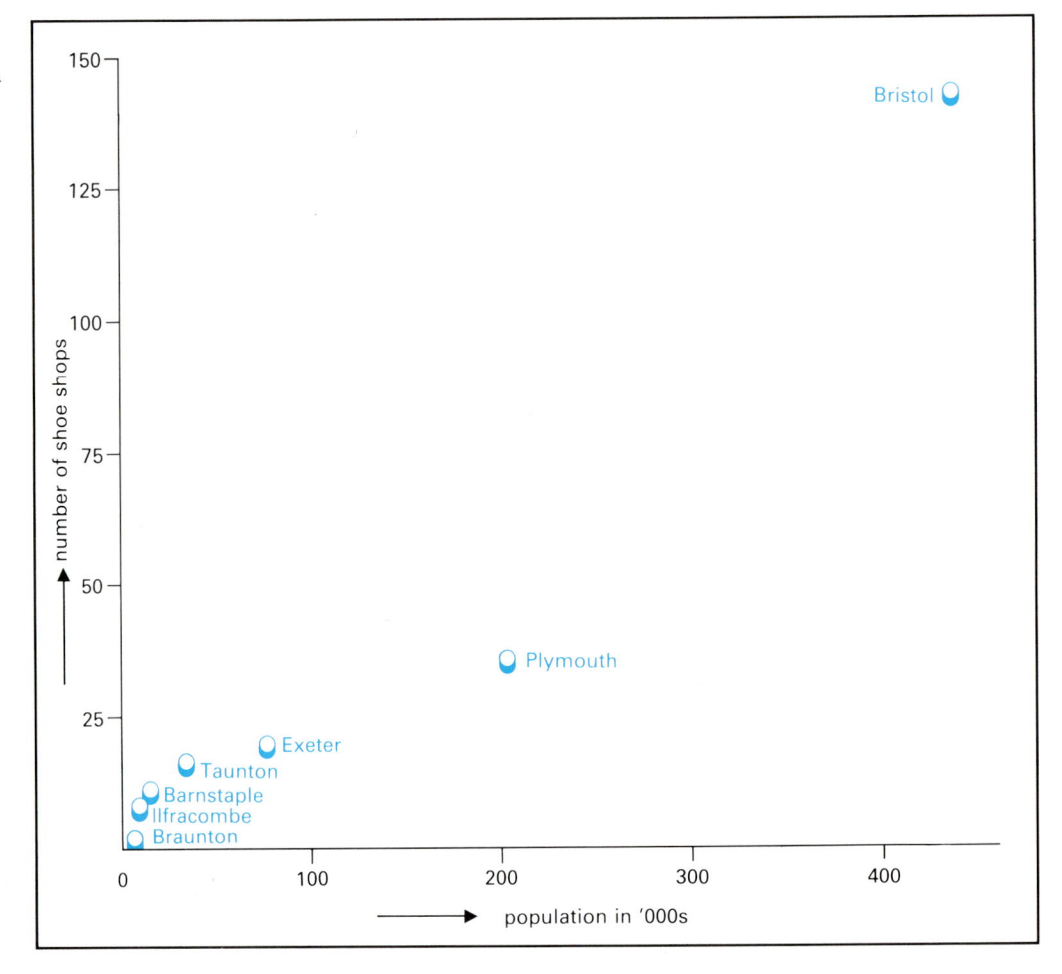

Fig. 123 Places of origin for grocery shoppers outside Braunton (sample survey only).

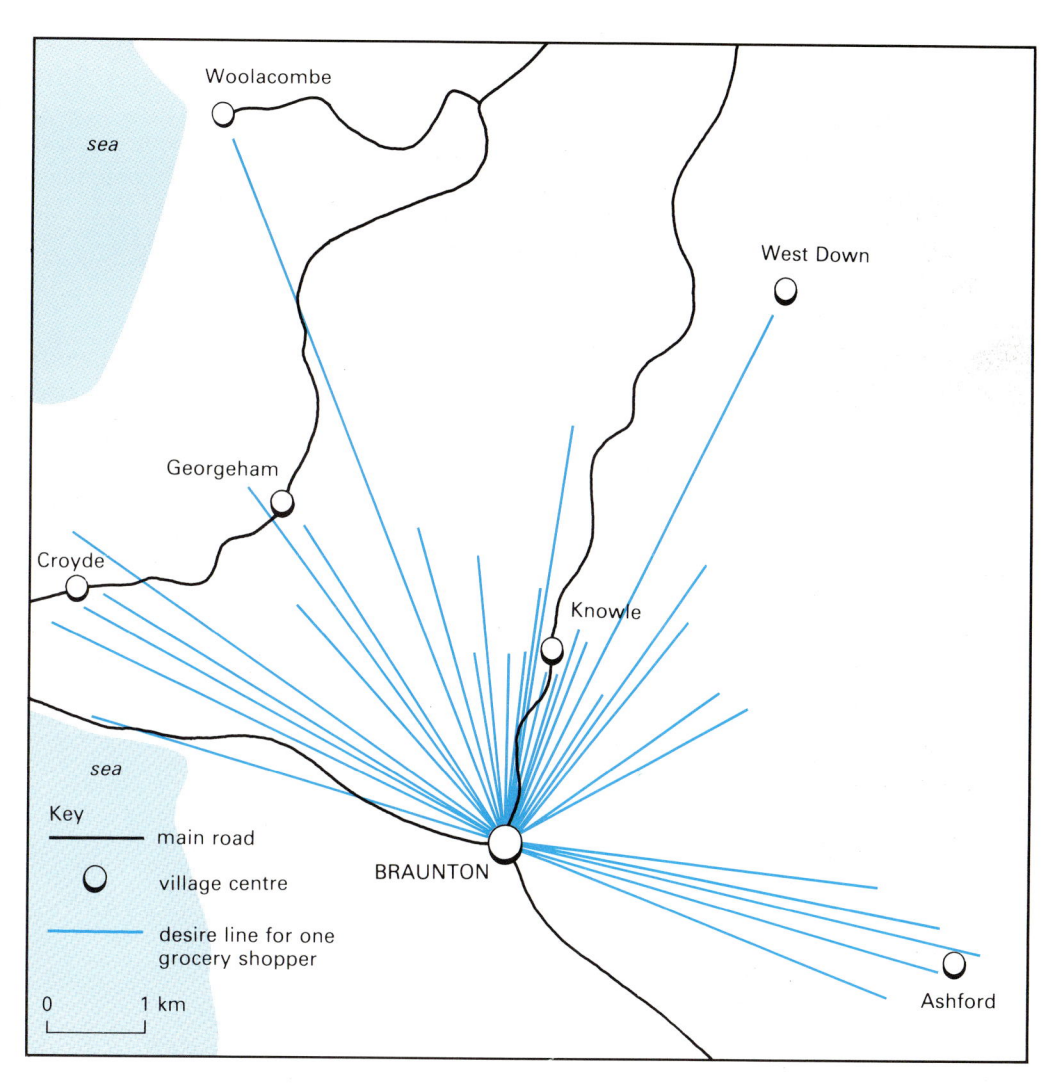

Fig. 124 North Devon: frequency of bus services per day.

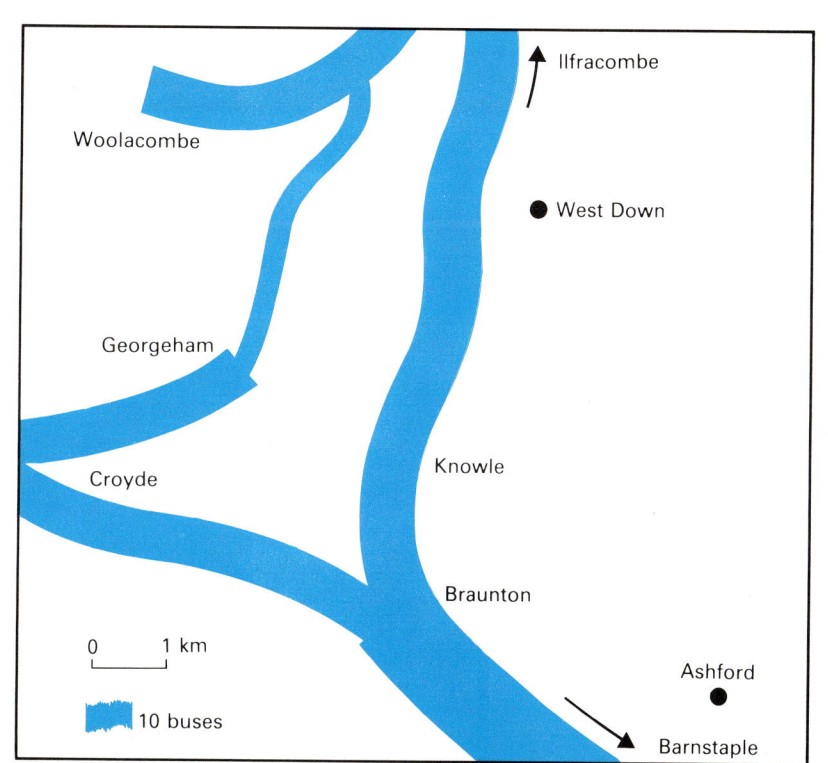

Photographs and sketches

Fig. 125 Thameshaven oil refinery from the west, oblique air photograph.

You have already made use of air photographs elsewhere in this book. They have been used largely as an aid to map interpretation to give you an alternative view, with different facts, of an area that you wish to study.

But geographers often make use of air photographs without maps. They are often used in the study of towns, but also in an attempt to understand very large industrial activities. Fig. 125 shows the huge Thameshaven oil terminal and refinery, with Canvey Island in the background.

1 Why are oil terminals and refinery facilities close together normally?
2 Can you name some of the other products of refining apart from petrol and oil?

The photograph is taken from above and to the west of Thameshaven. The River Thames flows out to the Channel in the far distance.

3 Give two reasons why the Thames is suitable for siting an oil refinery.
4 Explain why the discharging jetties are widely spaced and extend well out into the river.

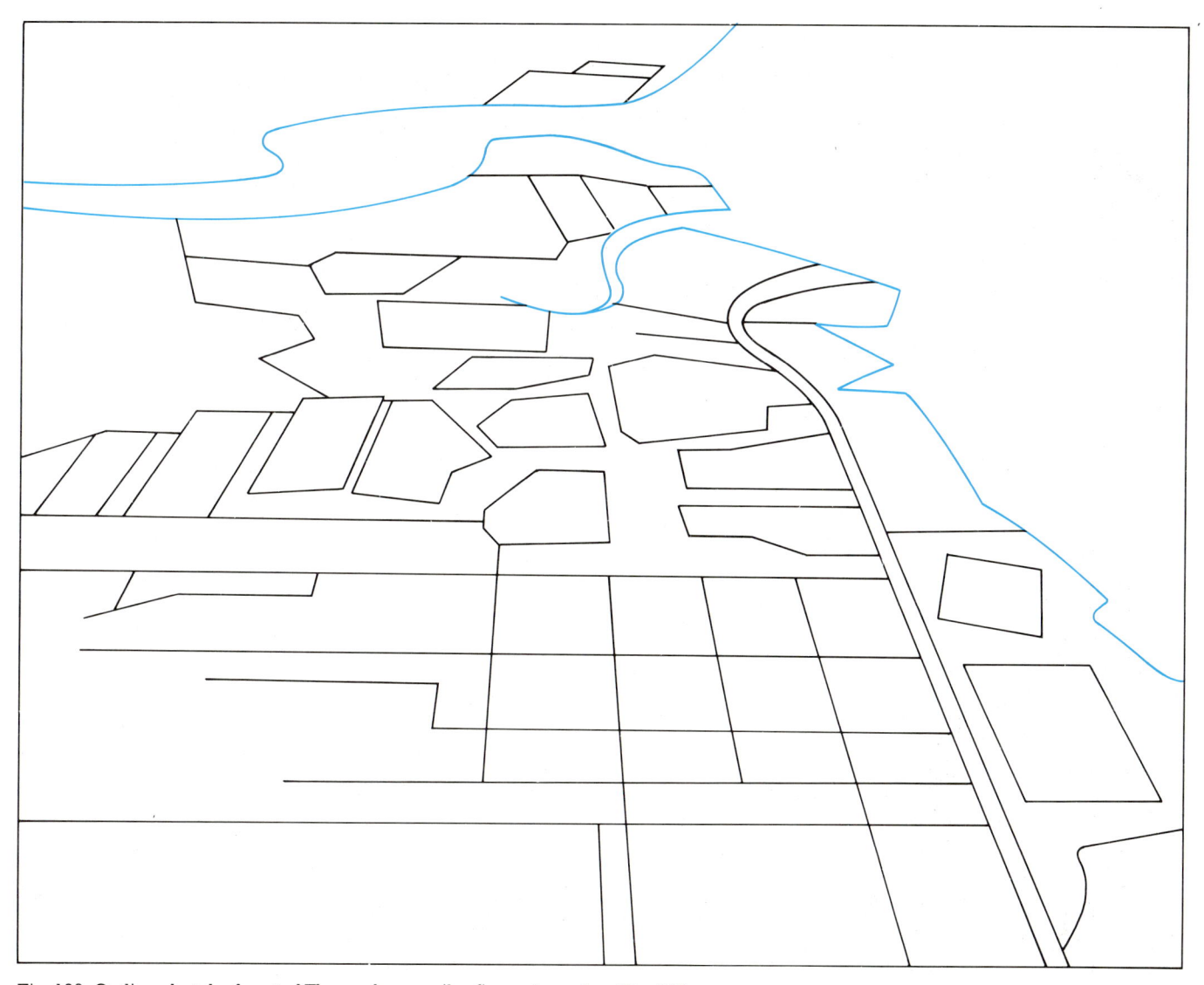

Fig. 126 Outline sketch of part of Thameshaven oil refinery, based on Fig. 125.

The major part of the area seems to be on very flat land, and much of it is occupied by storage tanks, though there are some areas occupied by different types of activity.

All the raw materials are brought in by sea. Some of the refined products are also taken out by sea, but most are taken out overland.

5 What do you think this land was used for before the terminal and refinery were built? Can you find evidence for your answer?
6 Why are there so many storage tanks and are they all used for the same product? Can you distinguish between storage, refining and administration areas? Why are they widely separated?
7 Why are some products taken out in smaller tankers by sea? Can you name three different methods of moving oil products overland? Which seems the most significant for Thameshaven?

Fig. 126 shows a sketch outline of part of the air photograph in Fig. 125. The artist has only drawn in the main trend lines from the photograph. This gives an opportunity to produce an annotated sketch.

8 Make a tracing of the sketch – leave it on the tracing paper and do not transfer it to your exercise book. Cut out the tracing neatly and stick it into your exercise book. Now shade in the following areas in different colours – transport facilities, storage tanks, refining facilities, administration areas, river, marshland, housing. Now look back over the answers to earlier questions in this section and annotate the sketch. That means you draw arrowed lines pointing to important features and write brief notes on each, as in Fig. 107.

News and views

Newspaper articles contain important geographical information, though they do tend to concentrate on rather sensational approaches. Nevertheless, it is important to understand the use of words and pictures, and to understand the problems that they highlight. Fig. 127 is an extract from a newspaper report relating to an oil disaster on the Brittany coast in March 1978.

1 What major factor caused the oil slick to spread as shown on the map?
2 Can you suggest the impact of such accidents on coastal environments? How might it affect local economies?
3 How could such accidents be avoided?

The second extract here (Fig. 128) comes from the *Daily Mirror*, 18 April 1985. It describes a pollution argument in the Humber Estuary in eastern England. This extract clearly shows two different viewpoints, and may also indicate a particular viewpoint held by the journalist and perhaps the newspaper.

4 Give a brief outline of the effect of waste from a chemical plant on the River Humber from the point of view of (i) fishing enthusiasts and (ii) the chemical firm.
5 Do you think the newspaper has reported this item in a completely balanced manner? Where do you think the newspaper's sympathies lie in this case?

The final extract Fig. 129 is an editorial comment on pollution. Editorial comments or leaders – as they are called – are intended to express a particular viewpoint rather than reporting facts.

6 Make a list of the pollution problems listed in the comment. Does it confirm your view of where the paper's sympathies lie in the account of the Humber Estuary? Do you agree with the comment? Would you add anything to it?

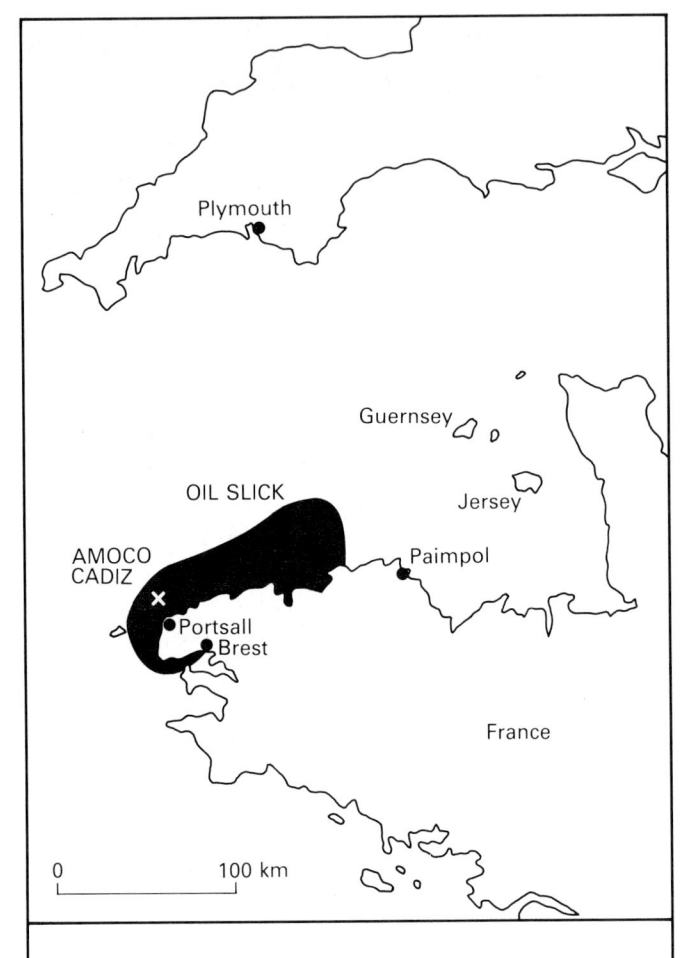

Oil disaster hits Brittany

In the worst oil pollution disaster ever recorded, the fully laden supertanker Amoco Cadiz was on March 16 forced onto rocks off Portsall, on the Brittany coast of France, after its steering gear failed, and gradually shed most of its load of 230,000 tonnes of crude oil into the sea, creating a huge oil slick which over the next two weeks heavily polluted more than 100 miles of French coast and threatened to move towards the Cornish coast, the Scilly Isles and the Channel Islands. The previous worst oil spillage had occurred in March 1967 when the Torrey Canyon tanker ran aground between the Scilly Isles and Land's End, spilling up to 60,000 tonnes of oil.

Fig. 127

Daily Mirror

Thursday, April 18, 1985 — FORWARD WITH BRITAIN — ★ 18p

THE LAST FISHERMAN

SHOCK ISSUE

BITTER: Bill Anderson was forced ashore

FISHERMAN Bill Anderson was the last of his line. He blames pollution for forcing him ashore after 57 years at sea.

Bill, 68, says bitterly: "I could have gone on till I was a hundred. It's that bloody factory. It's killed off everything.

"Nowadays there's not enough fish in there to pay for your tea after a day at sea."

The factory, on the edge of the River Humber at Grimsby, is owned by Tioxide UK, which makes titanium dioxide, the whitener in products like paint, plastic and toothpaste.

The firm makes a daily check and denies that there is a pollution problem.

But Bill is equally convinced of his case.

"People had been getting a good living out of this river for centuries," he says. "Then the factory went up in 1948 and my mates started going to the wall.

"The whelks disappeared, then the muscles. Even the barnacles have gone.

"The river's dead, totally dead."

About 40 boats were operating when the factory opened. Now it has all gone.

What gives them the right to dump all that stuff at sea?" he asks. "If they had dumped it on the land they would have been in jail in five minutes."

TIOXIDE pump up to 26,000 tons of waste into the Humber each day.

On a sunny day you can see it flowing bright orange for miles into the North Sea.

The plant's director, Ken Murphy, insists: "There is no pollution problem."

Fig. 128

DAILY MIRROR, Thursday, April 18, 1985

mirror Comment

WHEN WILL WE EVER LEARN?

LIVING BRITAIN CAMPAIGN

THE most terrible fact about deadly and daily pollution of our country is that we go on doing it even though we know the damage that it does.

WE poison the brains of our children with lead, knowing it will harm them for life.

WE tear up our hedgerows, knowing it means the inevitable destruction of British wildlife.

WE kill, we maim, we injure and no Government, no community and no national will is strong enough to stop doing it.

Destroy

But lead can be removed from petrol. Chemicals do not have to be emptied into rivers and streams.

● We need not let nuclear waste contaminate our beaches

● We do not have to pump acid rain into the atmosphere which will scar the fields and forests of Europe and Scandinavia.

● We damage and destroy for the sake of profit or personnel convenience. The loss of a species of birds may be shown as a profit in a farmer's accounts.

The waters around our shores are poisoned so that the bank balances of a factory on the land may look healthier.

We are not deliberate killers so much as thoughtless killers. We live in a unique land and yet we relentlessly eliminate what it is that makes it unique.

And we—each and every one of us—are to blame.

Fig. 129

EXAMINATION QUESTIONS (GCSE STYLE)

Map Extract 13

(*40 marks. The mark scheme and answers are provided for this set of questions on page 80.*)

1. (i) What difficulty would a cyclist face at 605042?
   (ii) What public service is available at Raisbeck (6407)?
   (iii) Give the length, in metres, of the railway cutting in square 6006.
   (iv) What is the difference in height between Holme House (658068) and Robin Hood's Grave (617107)?
   (*4 marks*)
2. State whether each of the following statements is true or false.
   (i) The railway serves Tebay.
   (ii) White areas on the map represent arable farmland.
   (iii) Orton village is on a hilltop.
   (iv) The road from Sunbiggin (659086) to Gaisgill (639054) is mainly downhill.
   (v) The map allows us to work out the number of deciduous trees in a wood.
   (vi) The track alongside Bowendale Beck (6702) is a public right of way.
   (*6 marks maximum*)
3. The following grid squares illustrate a variety of rural landscapes. For each one, describe the area and try to explain the land uses and settlement you find there:
   (i) square 6111 (ii) square 6510 (iii) square 6205.
   (*9 marks*)
4. Describe the chief features of the relief and drainage of the area between northings 06 and 12. (*7 marks*)
5. Explain to what extent road and railway routes have been influenced by the relief on the whole map extract. (*8 marks*)
6. The map extract shows many examples of changing patterns of settlement and communications over a long period. Write an account of the changes you have observed. (*6 marks*)

Map Extract 2

(35 marks)

1. What do you expect to find at:
   (i) 823204 (ii) 824195 (iii) 801182 (iv) 831215
   (v) 810180 (vi) 836177? (*3 marks*)
2. Give the distance in metres from the schools in square 8216 to Over Farm in square 8019 (i) in a straight line (ii) by road. (*2 marks*)
3. In what direction is the River Severn flowing at 804175? (*1 mark*)
4. (i) Is the A417 following a spur or a valley in square 8021?
   (ii) If you were facing NE at Manor Farm in square 8117 would you be looking uphill or downhill?
   (*2 marks*)
5. The area of water at 826205 is not a drinking water reservoir. What map evidence suggest this is true? (*2 marks*)
6. Which two forms of transport are likely to have influenced the siting of the 'Works' at 827177?
   (*1 mark*)
7. Much of the River Severn on this map is tidal.
   (i) What evidence on the map shows this?
   (ii) Give a grid reference for the place on (a) the west channel and (b) the east channel below which you expect the river to be tidal.
   (*3 marks*)
8. Describe the relief and drainage of the area covered by 8117 and 8118. (*6 marks*)
9. Describe, with relation to relief, the course of the railway (now disused) through squares 8119, 8019, 8020 and 8021). (*3 marks*)
10. Give a grid reference for a crossroads that you think is in the middle of the main shopping area of Gloucester. (*2 marks*)
11. Why do you think the area near Gloucester became such an important bridging point of the River Severn? (*2 marks*)
12. Suggest two reasons from map evidence for the success of the site of Longford (8320). (*2 marks*)
13. What do you suppose is the function of the 'Works' in square 8221? Give evidence for your suggestion. (*2 marks*)
14. Using map evidence compare the housing in Tredworth (8317) with that in Hempsted (8116, 8117.) (*4 marks*)

Map Extract 3

(20 marks)

1. Which of the following might affect your decision about living in square 5283:
   (i) the existence of a military training ground
   (ii) a busy main road
   (iii) the presence of unsightly extractive industry?
   A (i) alone   B (iii) alone   C (i) and (ii) only   D (ii) and (iii) only   E (i) (ii) and (iii)
   (1 mark)

2. If you were touring this area the facilities you would find in square 5084 would include:
   (i) a camp site
   (ii) a car park
   (iii) a castle open to the public
   (iv) an information centre.
   A (ii) alone   B (iii) alone   C (i) and (ii) only   D (ii) and (iii) only   E (iii) and (iv) only
   (1 mark)

3. Identify the following conventional signs:
   (i) NT at 505838   (ii) Arrowhead at 522752.
   (1 mark)

4. (i) Give the distance in metres, as the crow flies, from the church with a tower at Peter Tavy (5177) to the church at Brent Tor (4780).
   (ii) Give the direction between the same two points.   *(2 marks)*

5. Which is higher, Mary Tavy (5079) or Merrivale (5475)?   *(1 mark)*

6. Peter Tavy is a village. Give two pieces of map evidence which suggest this is true.   *(2 marks)*

7. Describe the layout of Peter Tavy.   *(3 marks)*

8. The car park in square 5375 was constructed for the National Park Authority. Give two reasons for the location of the car park, using map evidence.   *(2 marks)*

9. There are several military training areas ('Danger Areas') on this extract. Give two possible reasons for the location of these areas.   *(2 marks)*

10. (i) How far is it, in kilometres, by road from Peter Tavy Church to the hotel near Mary Tavy at 498798?
    (ii) Why is it so far?   *(2 marks)*

11. The drainage in the NE corner of the extract, bounded by easting 52 and northing 81, has been modified by human activity.
    (i) To which direction are the water courses in square 5282 flowing?
    (ii) Some of the water courses have been constructed (are not natural). What map evidence is there that suggests this is true?
    (iii) Where is the water that has been diverted from the natural drainage channels stored?
    (3 marks)

ANSWERS AND COMMENTS

Answers are provided only for some questions. Others should be discussed with your teacher.

Page
4   **4** 250 m   **5** 1:25 000, RF 1/25 000   **6** 0.5 km
6   **3** SO23
7   **4** C=4901, D=5100   **5** C=502014, D=509016
8   **3** (i) 804202 (B) (ii) 831188 (iii) 824187
     (iv) 824194 (C) (v) 826189 (vi) 818191
     (vii) 815198 (viii) 816189 (A) (ix) 827183
     (x) 824188 (xi) 814213 (xii) 821186 (xiii) 819195
9   **1** AS to CA 7 km, to Ho. 9 km, to M. 4 km and to Ha. 3
     0.5 km. CA to Ho. 4 km, to M. 3.5 km and to Ha. 6.5 km.
     Ho. to M. 7 km and to Ha 6.5 km. M. to Ha. 5 km.
     2 5.5 km
     3 AS to CA 8 km, to Ho. 12 km, to M. 8.5 km and to Ha.
     4.5 km. CA to Ho. 6.5 km, to M. 4.5 km and to Ha.
     8.5 km. Ho. to M. 11 km and to Ha. 9 km. M. to Ha.
     10.5 km.
     4 CA to AS 25 mins, to Ho. 20 mins, to M. 15 mins, to Ha.
     25 mins.
10   (All to nearest ha) **1** (i) 18 ha (ii) 8 ha (iii) 6 ha
     (iv) 20 ha **2** 8 ha between main roads.
     3 40 ha **4** 25 ha
11   **1** (i) S (ii) E (iii) NE (iv) WNW (v) SSE
     2 (i) N (ii) W (iii) SW (iv) ESE (v) NNW
     3 Land near Little Totham Hall **5** (i) 180° (ii) 90°
     (iii) 45° (iv) 292.5° (v) 157.5°
     6 As Ex. 5 above but + 6° in each case.
12   **1** 1 buildings 440388, 2 fenced tract/footpath,
     Milkaway Lane 448389, 3 farm 457377, 4 cliff, rock,
     coast 446377, 5 hotel 448377, 6 Saunton Court
     455379, 7 B-road 451376, 8 chapel 457376, 9 P
     457376, 10 sand/heath 448380
14   (1) railway (2) station (3) PO (4) A-road
     (5) telephone box (6) minor road (7) site of Roman
     villa (8) church (9) wood (10) pub
     (11) bridleway (12) footpath with right of way
     (13) path without right of way (14) railway bridge
     (15) mile post (x) 1.5 km to 2 km
15   The GR to the SW corner of Fig. 23 is SS 473316.
16   **1** (i) triangulation station (ii) spot height 115 m
     2 4979 cuttings, 5184 embankment
     3 (i) rock outcrop (ii) quarry
18   **3** (i) Fig. 34 (ii) Fig. 33 (iii) Fig. 32
20   **5** SW corner is 5075, 4 km by 4 km.
21   **6** (i) EF (ii) CD (iii) AB
24   **1** (a)–(ii), (b)–(iii), (c)–(i)
25   **5** 290 m to 390 m = 100 m in 1500 m = 1 in 15 (7% approx.) **6** (i) 1 in 5 (ii) 1 in 5 to 1 in 7
     9 concave **11** (ii) and (iii)
27   **1** ME 11 (a) 5462 (b) e.g. E 53 to 55, N 61 to 63;
     2 ME 1 and 2 (a) 806201 to 806205 (b) e.g. 803204;
     3 ME 14 (a) e.g. 437928 (b) e.g. 435934 (c) 4294;
     4 ME 7 e.g. 269065; **6** ME 7 (a) e.g. 265048
     (b) e.g. 264050 (c) e.g. 265043 to Red Tarn; **7** ME
     7 (a) 260082 (b) e.g. 252076 (c) e.g. 254080;
     8 ME 15 e.g. E 86 to 88, N 11 to 12.
29   **3** (i) village (ii) town (iii) hamlet **5** (i) village,
     village, village or hamlet, hamlet (ii) compact with
     'arms'; compact (triangle) with linear parallel 'back
     street'; compact; linear.
31   **9** Points to have noted: (i) On slopes of two small
     hills each about 60 m high, and on flatter land alongside
     N–S river estuary and in gap between hills. (ii) Tidal
     river site, town growing to north around headland to
     bay ('Skern'). (iii) Sheltered in valley and from W and
     SW gales by hills, but more open to NNE. (iv) Ferry
     crossing point and deeper water this side of estuary,
     water even at low tide. Main road from south, but no
     through routes. (v) Lifeboat station on headland,
     museum, near to Westward Ho! and country park.
     Probably picturesque with hills and sea views.
32   **2** Minor road untarred fenced; minor road untarred
     unfenced; minor road generally less than 4 m tarred
     fenced; minor road generally more than 4 m tarred
     unfenced on one side; minor road generally less than
     4 m tarred fenced; secondary road (B6261) fenced
     except for short stretch on left; main road (A685)
     fenced then unfenced on left after roundabout.
     4 (i) valley (ii) cuttings (e.g. 678052), embankments
     (e.g. 615054) (iii) embankments, bridges and short
     viaduct (612044) (iv) It follows a pass or gap between
     rock outcrops.
     9 Electricity transmission lines.
33   **10** Settlement, Cairn, Fort, Stone Row, Standing Stone,
     Stone Circle, Blowing Ho., Hut Circles, Cross, Tumulus,
     Coxtor.
35   **9** Possible interpretations (i) Ancient resistant rock
     (highland, heath, rivers) (ii) Clay/alluvium (flat,
     lowland, rivers) with sand/gravel 'terrace' above 152 m
     (dry) (iii) Sandstones? (undulating, rivers)
     (iv) Ancient resistant rock (highland, heath, outcrops,
     rivers) (v) Limestone or chalk (dry valley, no surface
     water, dip slope).

36 **3** (i) flowing from resistant to less resistant rocks (ii) drops suddenly down into U-shaped glacial valley after flatter upland (iii) source is slightly flatter marshy upland, more down-cutting when water has gathered into the mainstream (iv) steep drop from granite highland into deeper valley of River Tavy.
7 It crosses the watershed.

37 **12** (i) (78 cm) 19·5 km on 4 km² = 5 km/km² (ii) (8·5 cm) 4·25 km on 4 km² = 1 km/km² (iii) (80 cm approx – depends on measurement of meanders) 20 km on 4 km² = 5 km/km² (iv) (10 cm) 5 km on 4 km² = 1·25 km/km².

38 **6** Drumlins.

39 **1** (i) headland (erosion) (ii) bay (deposition) (iii) wave-cut platform (iv) 20 m approx. (vii) 50 m (viii) 500 m (ix) gulleys in the wave-cut platform.
2 About 8·5 km (to 460374) with climbs totalling about 60 m. So from Fig. 13 about 3 hours steady walking.

40 Map Search (i) (a) 3988 (b) 4687 (c) 4185 (ii) (a) 4384 (b) 4691 (c) 4390 (iii) (a) 4089 (b) 4583 (c) 4688 (iv) (a) 4388 (b) 4387 (c) 4383 (v) (a) 4084 (b) 4387 (c) 4685

46 **1** (iii) Radio and television links. (iv) Water, gas and oil pipelines underground.
4 (i) Kemsing – at least 4 km to travel to get onto M-way. M-way is in a cutting so may not be a noise (ii) West Kingdon – only 2 km on main road to access junction. M-way is on an embankment and may be visual and noise nuisance. Lead pollution, etc. will depend on local air currents etc.
8 (i) A38 from Tewkesbury District, A4173 Stroud, A40(T) Forest of Dean, A40(T) Cheltenham.
(ii) Cheltenham, Worcester, Bristol, Forest of Dean.
(iii) Certainly 835197, 834186, 828177, 832185.

47 **14** On the link between the Docks and the river (827185). **15** East channel – there are weirs across both east and west channels, but east channel can be entered through the locks above the weir from the canal and docks to travel upstream.

Mark scheme for examination question on Map Extract 13, page 76.

Acceptable answers (*Maximum marks 40*)

1 (i) Steep hill; hill; gradient; gradient 1 in 7 to 1 in 5 (0·5) (ii) Telephone (0·5) (iii) 500–550 m (0·5) (iv) 70 m (240 m to 310 m) (0·5)

2 (i) F (no station) (ii) F (iii) F (iv) T (v) F (vi) T (*6 for 6 correct, 3 for 5 correct, 1 for 4 correct, less than 4 correct 0 marks*)

3 (i) Highland 240 m to 320 m; mainly hilly with a little flat land at higher levels; steep-sided valleys; general north facing aspect; streams or small rivers; deciduous woodland, mainly in valley bottoms and on lower slopes; possibly rough pasture (sheep); no settlement now (tumulus); footpaths follow valley but keep to side slopes. (*3 marks – 4 × 0·5 + 1 for reasons for land use and settlement*)
(ii) Highland 270 m to 330 m; dry valley; scar/cliff/outcrop on NW side; north facing general aspect; probably limestone; road used as public footpath follows valley beneath scar; 'Ashby Winderwath' common land; probably rough pasture; no woodland or settlement. (*Marks as for 3(i)*)
(iii) Flat valley floor; mainly 180 m to 190 m; flood plain; river and tributary streams; hill to north; mainly south/SW aspect; main road on edge of flood plain; cuttings into valley side and bridges over tributaries; settlement mainly off flood plain; Coatflatt Hall on tributary's 'terrace' above main valley; building on minor (older) road parallel to main road and further off plain; one building on flood plain possibly barn?; probably pasture or, if well drained, arable. (*Marks as 3 (i)*)

4 **Relief**: south facing scarp, 100 m to 150 m in height, trending W to E, one particularly prominent section in squares 6409, 6509 rising from 250 m above SL to 400 m.
Highland to north of scarp; large exposures of rock (outcrops) in centre and east on higher land; no major gaps but several high level passes; plateau/dip slope dissected by S to N valleys.
Lower land to south of scarp; undulating (rolling hills) at general altitude 200 m to 270 m above SL; wide E to W valley of Tarn Sike and Rais Beck in eastern area; deeper N to S valley of Chapel Beck to west.
(*4 marks possible*)

Drainage: very little surface drainage to north of scarp except for NW corner with stream flowing to north; disappearing stream (680111).

Scarp forms spring line and several small streams flow south from base of scarp as tributaries to Rais Beck and Chapel Beck; several small lakes in Tarn Sike drainage basin; Tarn Sike itself disappears in square 6506 to reappear in 6406; scarp forms main watershed. (*3 marks possible*)

5 N–S routes have to cross two scarps and Tebay Fell. In the north the main scarp is crossed by roads at two places – the B6280 and a minor road both use high gaps at places where valleys are cutting back from the north. The lower scarp of Kelleth Rigg is crossed by roads following the N to S valleys of Chapel Beck (B6260) and Rais Beck (B6261), and by one minor road through Wain Gap (square 6505). Tracks across Tebay Fell follow smaller S to N valleys, but the A685, the motorway and the railway all follow the main gap of the N to S valley of the River Lune.

E–W routes mostly follow the Lune Valley (A685). The land between the scarps is undulating and routes are not so confined by relief. The main scarp with its rock outcrops is not as an easy land surface for E–W routes, nor is Tebay Fell with its deep S to N valleys.

The motorway, A road and railway all avoid steep slopes. (*8 marks*)

6 For full marks answers must illustrate change over time, and some mention of both settlement and communication. 'Some' changes are asked for, so complete coverage is not necessary for full marks.

Ancient settlement (settlements, castle folds, cairns, etc.) on highland in north, and near main river in gap (Castle Howe, Roman fort). Old Tebay also on river, Tebay (more recent) on terrace/hillside.

Communications – many N–S tracks that may have been more important in past times, Roman road up scarp in NW (6009). Modern roads (M-way and A685) use more engineering (cuttings, bridges, embankments) to reduce gradients and avoid sharp bends – compare with older B roads and minor roads. Railway – no station for Tebay – maybe closed and dismantled? (*6 marks maximum*)